TUBEWAY DAZE

THE UNTOLD STORY OF
TUBEWAY ARMY

Paul Goodwin

Acknowledgements

Printed in the U.K.

Published by JPG Productions.

Text copyright by Paul Goodwin ©2015

The moral right of the author, Paul Goodwin has been asserted.

Cover image by kind permission of classic rock and pop photographer Chalkie Davies.

Cover and layout design by Nick Robson.

Book title by Paul Goodwin
(with an invaluable tweak from Nick Robson).

Paul Goodwin and Nick Robson can both be reached via Facebook.

Nick Robson can be reached via his website:
www.livingtheamericandream.co.uk

All rights reserved.
No part of this publication may be reproduced, stored in a retrieval system or transmitted in any form or by any means, electronic, mechanical, photocopying or otherwise without the prior permission of the copyright owner.

Dedicated to the memory of Paul Gardiner
1958 – 1984

"Gary already had it all planned out. He told me he was going to have this hit with a song called 'Cars' and this was years before he'd actually written the music. When 'Are 'Friends' Electric?' became a big success, he said that the order had gone wrong and it wasn't supposed to happen that way."
Gerald Lidyard

"Gary's ambitions were well beyond the ambitions of most punk bands that were happy to play a good gig and have a few beers in the bar. Gary wanted to be a star like Bowie."
Steve Webbon

"I did have a vague kind of master plan but it was never as well thought out or as detailed as people seemed to believe. I pretended at the time because I wanted people to think that I was on top of things."
Gary Numan

"Paul and Gary complemented each other. Paul was a good solid right-hand man."
Steve Webbon

"*Tubeway days now seem quite unreal.*"

Author's note:

Gary Numan's four huge worldwide hits in 1979, first with 'Are 'Friends' Electric?' and *Replicas* and then later that year as a solo artist with 'Cars' and *The Pleasure Principle*, will be forever burnt into the minds of fans and dominate his unique career as far as music biographers and historians are concerned. But it is also important to note that his meteoric rise to pop superstar status was no overnight success. Prior to the band's groundbreaking success, Tubeway Army was in essence, just one of hundreds of punk and new wave bands regularly playing the smaller venues around central London towards the end of the 1970s.

Together with loyal ally Paul Gardiner, the duo dutifully gigged their way around the London punk clubs in a variety of changing line-ups. This was before Gary's accidental discovery of a Moog synthesiser in the spring of 1978 that changed everything about their direction and future.

This chance encounter with a forgotten synthesizer set the wheels in motion that would alter both Gary and Paul's lives forever, setting them on a path that would ultimately lead to worldwide fame and superstardom.

Tubeway Daze, the untold story of Tubeway Army, lifts the lid on these pre-success years, revealing a fascinating story that has become the very stuff of music legend.

Paul Goodwin, 2015.

CREDITS

To build this manuscript's initial framework, we've cross-referenced both Ray Coleman's and Steve Malins' excellent Gary Numan autobiographies, as both featured important information that was crucial to the creation of this book. Further archive material and commentary found throughout this manuscript came from the following sources: the *Images* interview albums of the late 1980s, Gary Numan's *Alien* magazine, Stephen Roper's *Back Stage*, various internet biographies, rare newspaper and online interviews, social media enquiries and interviews conducted via email with this author, as well as my own previously published works concerning Gary Numan and Tubeway Army; the *Electric Pioneer* and *Tracks* books. Some of the comments included here have been edited slightly with less relevant information being set aside. All comments though, are entirely genuine and have been associated with the source wherever possible.

Despite all of the above, this book would simply not have turned out the way it has, had it not been for the valued input of Nick Robson. Nick is a long time friend of Gary and his family and is the author of the successful 2007 book *Living The American Dream*? Nick has graciously guided this project throughout and I am forever indebted to him for being kind enough to take time out of his busy life to oversee each part of this story to make sure it was historically accurate and correct. Nick also helped breathed new life into the text which really took the entire project to a completely new level. For more information about Nick and his own successful career, please visit the website www.nureference.co.uk and search for Nick Robson in the interview section.

I must also thank Annette Gardiner, who placed her trust in me to bring her own unique, never before heard story out into the light.

And lastly kudos must also go to Gerald Lidyard and to Martin Mills and Steve Webbon of Beggars Banquet who collectively must have winced and groaned when they received yet another email from an aging Numanoid with a list of 'questions' for them…

TUBEWAY DAZE

THE UNTOLD STORY OF TUBEWAY ARMY

INTRODUCTION

"See the strange boy keeping to the shadows"

(Lyric taken from the Tubeway Army song 'Friends')

September 1979

He sits alone backstage, slumped against a flight case, head bowed, deep in thought. Beyond the curtain, a packed auditorium explodes in a maelstrom of screaming voices calling out his name. This was the moment he and long time collaborator, Paul Gardiner, had always dreamed about. The meticulous planning, the sacrifices, the struggles; all of it had led to this one singular moment in time. With the mild panic beginning to subside, he finally stands, takes a deep breath and without looking back, walks triumphantly towards the stage.

Life for these two 21-year-olds, who together had dared to dream of being stars, would never be the same again…

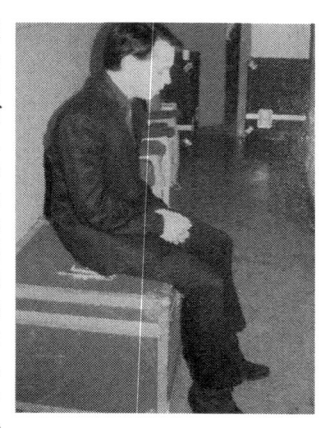

Backstage moments before taking to the stage at Glasgow Apollo 20th September 1979.

1977

CHAPTER 1
THE BEGINNING

"I'm growing tired of this place, I think it's time to change my face"
(Lyric from 'Oh! Didn't I Say')

On a cold, damp English day in January 1977, 19-year-old Gary Anthony James Webb gathered together a group of like-minded individuals with the intention of forming his first band. Although he'd previously played in a number of short-lived semi-pro groups in an around his home town of Ashford in Middlesex, this venture was going to be the real thing. With punk rock reinventing the British music business during the late 1970s, getting into a band had become almost a rite of passage for every teenager hooked on the buzz-saw three-chord punk movement ruled at that time by The Sex Pistols, The Damned and The Clash.

"In 1977 I started a punk band with some mates," revealed Gary when speaking to Steve Malins in 1997 for his book *'Praying To The Aliens'*, *"the drummer was an old school friend called Kenny Bishop and the bass player was a David Bowie look-alike called Henry Sabini. We had another guitar player called Neville Nixon. Neville was a coke fiend, he could hardly start a conversation without a line of coke."*

According to Ray Coleman's 1982 autobiography of Gary Numan, both Sabini and Nixon had been discovered and recruited via the musician's personal grapevine. With the other members of the group being fairly inexperienced as players and writers, Gary quickly found himself assuming the position of leader. *"I was the only one who had written any songs and the only one who was interested in writing any songs so I became the front man, vocalist and songwriter. I bought the drummer his kit; I showed the bass player how to play bass. In fact I* borrowed my Uncle Gerald's bass guitar. It was great at the time as they were all my friends and I was writing the songs because nobody else wrote any, and it was good."

Gary had left college a year earlier, to the dismay of his parents and in particular his father, Tony Webb, who demanded to know what his plans were, now that he had abandoned full time education. *"He would say to me things like, 'What are you gonna do?' and I would say, 'I'm going to be a famous rock 'n' roll star, Dad.' I can remember clearly when he said, 'Ah good. That'd be nice, wouldn't it?'"*

Gerald Lidyard, Gary's uncle, remembers this period well. *"Before Tubeway Army, I remember Gary telling me that he was going to be a pop star, I don't think his parents were too pleased about it and they sent him round to me for a chat. I'd been a working musician for several years so I thought if I talked about the realities of life in a group, that I might put him off. Or, if he was serious about it, he would knuckle down and work at his music rather than just carry on dreaming about it."*

But Gary did work at it, and with absolute determination. With Gerald enlisted, they recorded a little-known and mostly unheard demo tape of four of Gary's sci-fi tinged songs at a tiny 4-track recording studio in Cobham, Surrey in 1976. *"I remember going to a studio in Cobham a couple of years before we did the demo for 'That's Too Bad',"* Lidyard confirmed, *"I think Gary was still at college at the time and even back then we recorded his songs. He was never interested in playing cover versions. I don't recall the tracks or titles, but I think that at least one of tracks became either 'My Shadow In Vain' or 'Oh! Didn't I Say'. I remember unearthing the cassette from this session a couple of years ago, so I am positive this all took place. Unfortunately I have since buried the cassettes again! This was not Gary's only foray incidentally, when he was about sixteen or seventeen, he had previously done a short performance with a pub/cabaret band that I was playing with (who were very much well worn veterans and not particularly encouraging to him), followed by a few wedding / Working Man's Club type gigs with Richard (my cousin, Gary's second cousin)."*

"The very, very first one I did was in a little garage studio," Numan confirmed in a later interview, *"I believe it was called Salsifi Studios. She had a bloke who built it in this garage. Gerald went with me. We did four songs during a three hour session, one of which ended up being on the first album. That was my first introduction to it."*

"Around 1973 it was clear to see that Gary was probably going to make his career in music as an artist," remembered Nick Robson in an interview with NuReference, *"he started changing the colour of his hair, experimenting with make-up and dressing pretty differently and I guess the rest of us did pretty much the same thing at that time. The way we*

presented ourselves was suddenly extremely important and we wanted to be different to what was on offer in the high street. The one shop we used to visit frequently was Shelley's in Carnaby St. for shoes, and we also used to go to Kensington Market where you could buy very different clothes that just weren't available anywhere else. This was before any of us could drive so on Saturdays, for the price of a Red Rover bus ticket we could travel anywhere and everywhere in London for an entire day for 25p."

With his music career beginning to gain momentum and his father's frustration temporarily appeased, Gary's next port of call after his early college exit, had been the local Job Centre where he shared his ambitions during his first visit. *"I want to be a rock-n-roll star, I want to be famous."* Inevitably, the interviewer at the Job Centre told him he was on his own as far as pop stardom was concerned. But undeterred by the man's disappointing response, Gary painstakingly mapped out to him the route he was going to travel in order to reach his goal.

In 1986, when talking to writer Peter Gilbert, Gary revealed how the conversation with the man at the Job Centre went that day. *"I'm going to advertise and I'm going to do auditions and join bands, I'll find a working band, and he said, 'Fine'. And for the next six months he let me do whatever I wanted. He didn't send me off to any interviews or anything. And he really sort of like, backed me and he let go out and do it, which was great."*

But however confident and assertive Gary may have appeared that day, the truth was that the shy teenager was merely acting out a part, appearing completely at ease in front of an audience when in reality, he was the polar opposite. *"I was quite insular. I wasn't a big 'going out' person. So I would spend most of my time indoors, on my own. I didn't have a lot of mates. I was just dreaming about being in a band. I wrote a lot of songs back then and that's pretty much all I did from when I was an early teenager."*

Although the Job Centre interviewer may have given Gary the green light to do whatever he wanted, his father Tony was by now growing weary of the situation, eventually losing his patience. Finally, he took steps to confront his daydreaming son.

"It was a lecture from my Dad that really got me off my backside. You see, he was a baggage handler at Heathrow and worked hard and had three jobs when I was young," remembered Gary, "One day he turned on me and he said, really inciting me, he said, 'You're just going to shit! You've done nothing! You're blowing out school. You're blowing out college. You haven't got a job. You're doing nothing. You're sitting on your arse doing nothing. All you ever do is talk about it and dream about it. You aren't going to do anything. You're a waste of time!' And he said he was sick of it. Now, it really came as a shock and a jolt to my system, and so I got off my backside. The very next day I started advertising and doing something about it. And I think within a couple of weeks I was in a band and working. And then my Dad, and bearing in mind he was just a working-class bloke, he worked at British Airways as a lorry driver, or so I'm told - he bought me a really, really lovely guitar. (Gibson Les Paul) It was a lot of money in those days, a real lot of money, like a month's wages at that point. And he bought me a nice amplifier too. He bought me the gear I needed to go out and start playing. And he's been like that throughout. He bought me a PA system and a van, all with the pretence of me paying him back, but he never took any money back for it. I lived in the house virtually for nothing. My Mum and Dad were great from the very beginning, I owe them everything."

Unfortunately, none of the groups Gary joined lasted very long and he was quickly beginning to grasp the limitations of the British Legion and WMC circuit. *"I just thought if you joined a band you played around a bit and then somebody discovered you and you became famous. I was fifteen, sixteen when I first started doing this. And, yeah I really was that naïve. That's how I thought you did it. And then it slowly dawned on me that playing British Legions wasn't going to get me famous. And I certainly wasn't going to get famous for doing 'Route 66' or 'Satisfaction' and 'Tie A Yellow Ribbon'. So I decided then that I really ought to start concentrating on my own songs. I needed to start working in a different area at different clubs, I needed to start bringing myself to an audience where the people were that could make you famous, where the pressmen were, where the A&R men were. The A&R men don't go to British Legions; they go to the Marquee and places like that, the London clubs and various clubs around the country. But it did take some time for that to dawn on me, really. The only reason I got in to some of those bands is because my Dad had bought me a good guitar. And so they let me in because I had great gear. When they had heard me, they'd send me out the back and tell me I'd been turned down."*

CHAPTER 2
MEAN STREET

"Seems like I outgrew my station, sweet young boys turning green"

(Lyric taken from 'Mean Street')

(Photo ©1977 Chris Beat)

Having finally grown weary of the working man's pub rock circuit, Gary hit upon the idea of perhaps forming a band of his own where he could at last perform his own material. However, any lingering doubts about the hazy plans he may have had about his future life, were immediately brushed aside in the autumn of 1976. This resulted from an electric and memorable Sex Pistols performance that Gary witnessed with friends on 15th November at the Notre Dame Hall (now the Leicester Square Theatre) in Central London. *"I got hassled by Billy Idol at that gig the Pistols did,"* Numan later recalled, *"I thought he was going to beat me up!"*

But the show itself would prove to be a defining moment in Gary's life as the formation of his first band began to finally take shape.

Speaking to Ray Coleman in 1982, Gary explained the reasoning behind the

5

importance of forming his own group rather than joining an established one. *"I'd practiced with and auditioned for so many bands that had come to nothing, I decided I could do no worse than have a crack at my own. At least if I wrote a song, I could play it."*

That first band, with its short-lived name, Riot, eventually made its official live debut in early 1977 at Crackers nightclub, a venue located on Wardour Street in London's Soho district. The band later performed a second show at Stanwell Village Hall near Heathrow (with a hasty name change to Heroin) and then a third gig sometime later at Ashford Grammar School in Middlesex, but reborn once again, this time as Stiletto. The income generated from each show ranged from £10 to £15.

"I vaguely remember the first time I saw Gary perform in a band in front of an audience.' Nick Robson remembered, *'I think it was in Stanwell Village Hall, close to where we all lived and I remember that they had a bass player who was the double of David Bowie, straight out of The Thin White Duke era. If I remember correctly, his name was Henry Sabini. I don't think I was more than 15 or 16, but for all of us there that night, the gig was unbelievably exciting, the band playing what seemed to us at the time, brilliant versions of Lou Reed's 'White Light, White Heat' and 'Waiting For The Man'. On the night, it felt like a packed venue, but thinking back now, there were probably only around forty people in the audience, if that. What hit me on that night, was that I suddenly realised Gary had enormous stage presence and the girls loved him so I knew immediately that he was going to be a rock 'n' roll star."*

Changing the band's name, which Gary had originally chosen, had been at the insistence of the other band members who had slowly started objecting to Gary's growing dominance within the group.

"All of a sudden, the ego started to rear its head," explained Gary in 1986 to Peter Gilbert, *"and the band started saying things like, 'You're doing everything. Why are you doing everything? Why are you singing and writing the songs?' And I said, 'Because none of you want to do anything and in the six months we've been together, none of you have written any songs. That's why. You see, if you want to go out and do a gig, you've got to play songs.' I said, 'You haven't written anything. What do you want me to do?'"*

The band's response was one of apathy and Gary later recalled the way he was perceived by his peers during his mid to late teens. *"Up until that point I had just been one of the lads in this crowd of people and very much one of the less important ones if you like. In any group of people, you have your big ringleaders and the blokes who think they're in charge of it all and they say where you're going to go that night. And I was just one of the blokes at the back. And all of a sudden I started to become a little bit more important. And we're talking about a very, very minor level* here. But within the group I had to become more important; I started to become the main one. I was the bloke in the band and the band did become the main thing of that group of people; they followed it around everywhere. It started becoming the main talking point. And so, all of a sudden, I started to become a little bit too important within it, which is hard to understand because it was really at just such a tiny level and I was so surprised that such a thing could happen amongst friends."

Keen to keep the peace though, Gary vividly recalled offering his band members a compromise during that early band meeting. *"I said, 'All right, then. We won't do any of my songs. We'll do all yours. So go and get them.' And they didn't; they didn't have any songs. But they couldn't quite qualify that. I was told that it was because I did all the writing and it was stopping them doing more popular stuff at gigs. I said at the time 'You can't do gigs and get anywhere in the long run without new songs. Somebody's got to write new stuff. I've got a dozen and you haven't got any. We'd better use mine until you write some.' I didn't intend at the time to become a big front-man pop star anyway, I was just doing it to gain experience."*

This uncomfortable situation didn't last long. A mutinous band meeting saw Gary's role within the group being greatly diminished. *"They said they didn't want me writing the songs and they didn't want me doing all the singing anymore and when I asked why they didn't do some, they said they didn't want to. They said they wanted to get someone else in to do the singing instead."*

The secret plan by his band-mates to replace him as lead vocalist eventually came to fruition at a later rehearsal when Gary found himself sharing the microphone with another man called Jeremy Harrington. Gary later recalled that particular day to Steve Malins, *"One day I went along to a rehearsal in Chelsea and when I got there I was surprised to hear someone else singing. A weird couple of hours followed with this man and me trying to outdo each other by both shrieking into the one microphone at the same time."*

Things finally came to a head in early May when the band arranged to go and watch a local group together and as Gary was the only one who had a driving licence and a car, he took on the task of going round to the other members' homes to collect them.

"I used to be the Joe idiot that used to drive them everywhere in my car for nothing," seethed Gary in 1986, *"One day I turned up to pick them up and they weren't there, they'd gone without me; we were all supposed to be going to the Rock Garden in Covent Garden to see a band so I went to the club where we were supposed to be going, and nobody would talk to me, not one single person. I went up to them and said, 'Oh, hello. I thought I was supposed to be picking you up.' And they said,*

'Yeah, well . . .' And they walked off. That was that. Not a word. Even the girlfriends wouldn't talk. Then one of the girlfriends later came up and said they didn't want me in the band anymore. Not only was I out of the band, I was out of the entire circle of friends. I was stunned. It obviously had been planned for some time, this dissent if you like, amongst them all. And I really couldn't understand it at all. I was really upset at the time; the whole band and their friends and girlfriends completely sent me to Coventry; they dropped me from parties, from anything at all. It was petty jealousy of the fact that I was singing and writing, but jealousy at such a small level. I was furious."

With Gary out of the way, the remaining members carried on with Harrington supplying the vocals and of course, the group's name changed once again for the fourth time, finally becoming the soon to be doomed Mean Street. *"They weren't called Mean Street until after they had gotten rid of me,"* stated Gary, *"they went out and did their own set and they had a couple of my songs in it anyway. I was disgusted. And all my so-called friends at the time would follow them around religiously and pogo at every gig. It was like rent a crowd."*

CHAPTER 3
PAUL GARDINER

"Just my steel friend and me, I stand brave by his side"
(Lyric taken from 'Steel And You')

Summer 1977

While the Sex Pistols sat 'invisibly' at number one in the British singles chart with their anarchic Jubilee-decrying anthem 'God Save The Queen', Gary's former band-mates in Mean Street eagerly threw themselves into a schedule of live work. Many of their gigs, which took place at The Roxy, were as support act to embryonic versions of bands like Adam And The Ants and The Police, among others. For Gary though, who was still angry with his sudden and traitorous expulsion from the band, self-pity did not linger long in his mindset.

In early June he began feverishly scouring the small ads in the national music press, looking for another band to join. *"I thought I'd just join a band,"* Gary explained to Peter Gilbert in 1987, *"work in the background a little bit, get experience and start to move forward again."* Fortunately, he quickly found what he was looking for when an ad seeking a guitarist caught his eye in *Melody Maker*. When he called the number provided, he spoke for the first time with Paul Gardiner, who told him that auditions for his band were taking place at a club in West Drayton in Middlesex and he was welcome to come along.

Paul was born on 1st May, 1958 to Alec and Doris Gardiner and had previously been a student at Barnhill Community High School in Hayes. *"Paul's only job to date at the time, was as a church organ tuner apart from much earlier in his childhood when he worked as a milkman's helper,"* revealed Paul's then girlfriend Annette Gardiner.

On the day the auditions were due to begin, Gary arranged to meet Paul and drive them both to the club. *"I got on with Paul straight off. I picked him up and he took me to where the audition was and on the way there we were sort of chatting away, smashing bloke, lots of similar interests and things. So by the time we got to the audition he was sort of an ally. Paul had been doing the singing in the band up until that point. Anyway, I did the audition and some other people came in and did their auditions. I don't think the other two blokes in the band were particularly keen on me. One yelled, 'Shouldn't have bothered!' I did have good gear though that my Dad had bought me, so that was a factor. But Paul was very keen on me being in. He didn't want me in the band for my guitar prowess which wasn't that good really but he could see something else in me."*

Paul later confirmed this, *"The band was hardly off the ground when Gary came to the audition. The others couldn't see his difference but I thought he was exceptional at playing guitar - like nobody else did at that level in 1977. But I was the only one who wanted Gary in the band."*

For Gary though, being a front-man again was the furthest thing from his mind, intent on just playing his guitar and letting someone else take centre stage. *"When I joined The Lasers I'd had enough of problems. I was determined to just join another band and this time simply be a guitarist and stand in the background because of the problems I'd had with Mean Street. Becoming the front person of a band seemed to attract quite a lot of hostility and jealousy so I didn't want any more of it. I wanted to gain experience; I didn't want to keep having arguments with people, because as soon as I detect any ill feelings behind the scenes I'd rather just pull out and leave it."*

But no matter how hard Gary tried to suppress and stifle his natural leadership qualities, they couldn't be hidden completely or indefinitely and neither could his strong personality.

"Well, Gary got the job," said Paul, *"and then the trouble began. We did a rehearsal and the songs that Gary brought in were totally different from anything we'd been doing. I was the band's singer at this stage but the way Gary sang was just unique so I told the others I was happy to give up singing and let him be the front man. The drummer and the other guitarist couldn't agree with me. They asked for a private meeting with me and they told me he had no potential. I said they were wrong; he was so different that we had to take him and his songs and go along with his ideas. I was convinced from the first hearing that he was going to get somewhere."*

"We started to play some numbers in rehearsal and Paul was doing the singing." Gary revealed to Peter Gilbert in 1987, *"Which was okay; he could sing all right. Bit of a strain on some notes. So I said, 'Do you eventually want to be doing your own stuff?' and they said, 'Yeah, we want to, but we haven't got any.' They were doing punk versions of 1960s songs like 'Day Tripper', quite fun but not going anywhere. And I said, 'Well I've got this tape with some songs I wrote for this other group and if you want to, you can start doing some of them, it would be a start to us having our own repertoire.' So I played them the tape and they just started doing all of those songs. That day The Lasers and I began preparing a complete set. Eventually Paul said, 'You'd better do the singing because I can't do anything like that.' And he wasn't that interested in being the front man, never was. He was quite happy just to*

be there playing his bass. So within a week I was back to square one again, singing at the front, writing songs."

It was now the middle of June and with a new band behind him, Gary set about trying to schedule some live work. First attempt was at a club in Covent Garden called The Roxy, which held regular auditions for up-and-coming new bands. The Roxy sprang to life on New Years Eve of 1976 and was once the home of a failing gay club called Chagueramas. The venue was sited in Neal Street, an area populated by rundown fruit and vegetable warehouses. As a club it didn't hold much appeal. On the ground floor, where the bands performed to their peers and competitors, the ceiling had long since been ripped down and the upstairs reception room which housed a small bar was little better. In truth the club was dirty, dark and frankly, quite nasty.

"The Roxy was in decline after the first three months," recalled DJ Don Letts, *"basically the best groups were starting to make it big and we were getting the dregs down there."*

On his arrival at The Roxy, Gary spotted a poster advertising his former band Mean Street, scheduled to play a support role in a few days time to Australian punk band, The Saints, on 26th June. Although unhappy at the idea of meeting his old band again, Gary made his way inside because the ad had given him an idea that could provide an opening for his own band. His idea was to put forward his band, The Lasers, as the support act for Mean Street and he was fairly surprised when the idea was met with a positive reaction from the club manager at The Roxy. Unfortunately, there was a pretty unsavoury caveat that came with the deal. The man in question, Kevin St. John, was less than bashful when he told Gary that he wanted to have sex with him in return for The Lasers getting a chance to play at the club. St. John quickly backtracked when Gary retold the story to Mean Street, but oddly, still offered to add The Lasers as a second support act to the upcoming Saints/Mean Street show.

Kevin St John

Gary later confirmed: *"The man who owned the club thought it'd be a real laugh to put us on the same night and not say anything, so he was all in on it. He thought it would be great fun. We practiced and practiced and practiced and it was good on the night. So the first show we ever did was with Mean Street; we were still called The Lasers and we were at the bottom of the bill but we went up and did our bit."*

After the show though, Gary's former band-mates from Mean Street angrily confronted the singer.

"They were actually annoyed because I hadn't told them I was in the band, as if I owed them anything," recalled an incredulous Gary, *"It was diabolical what they did. It really was. And then to have the cheek to tell me that I had betrayed them for not telling them I was in a band. I couldn't believe that kind of hatred. We blew them apart; they were not very good at all."*

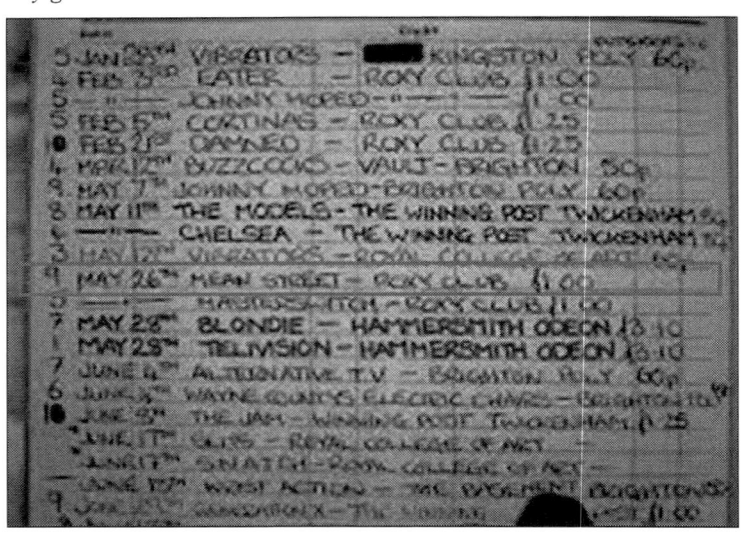

That night, returning home from the gig, Gary and Paul drove past the Hammersmith Odeon together for the first time. Both remembered having a personal affinity with the venue, particularly Gary, later revealing the mantra that both he and Paul followed. almost religiously.

"We always used to say 'one day.' And it got to be a little pattern because that to me was always like the best gig in the world. If you had played Hammersmith Odeon, then you'd made it. That was success. We'd always say every time we went past it, 'one day' that we'd be there."

Talking to *Digital Spy* magazine in 2014, Gary reiterated what he'd said all those years ago about the importance of the Hammersmith Odeon, *"When I was a kid growing up, that was the place that I went to see most of the bands. I just sat in the audience dreaming that one day it would happen for me. So it's always retained a special sort of feeling for me and the fact that I was born in Hammersmith added to the emotion."*

At around the same time as the Roxy performance, Gary's natural assertiveness led him to begin questioning the band's name during a conversation with Paul and the other Lasers members. In 1987 he recalled the discussion he'd had with the rest of the band, to Peter Gilbert. *"You ever notice that the punk bands are all called 'the somethings'? Why not call ourselves something other than 'the somethings' and Paul said, 'What do you suggest?' So I said, 'I just happen to have here a whole selection of names which you might be interested in.' It was Paul who picked Tubeway Army. So that's how it came to be called Tubeway Army. That sorted the name out."*

The band's new name actually came from a fictitious planet, part of an idea that Gary had abandoned writing about as a youth. In this imaginary world, everyone lived in futuristic cities under huge glass domes and each army-patrolled city was linked by travel tubes, in short 'a tubeway army.'

However, as Gary was settling into his new leadership role within the band, fate once again intervened.

"We had a gig coming up; we were only doing like one about every fortnight so at the time it was quite important. We had a practice planned and one of the boys who had been in charge of the band before I came along just cancelled it, just like that. So I got a bit annoyed about this, and I said, 'You can't cancel this, it's important for us, we need the practice.' He said, 'Well I didn't have any money, it was two quid and I couldn't afford it.' I didn't like his attitude when I started to question him about it; he sort of said I was the last to join the band and not to come on so heavy. I was doing all the songs and all the arranging but he took the attitude that I was a kid. So I said, 'You really should have spoken to us, there are four of us in it and it's important for all of us. And if it was only two quid I would have given you two quid just so we could have had the practice.' Then a few more things were said and it became obvious that it was happening again because I had gone to the front. So I said to Paul, 'I've had enough of this. I'm off.' And I was a little bit childish about it; I said, 'Tubeway Army's my name, I'm going to take it with me.' And Paul said, 'No, I've had enough too so I'll come with you.' Paul said he didn't like the drummer and guitarist anyway and that seemed to be the end of it. Me and Paul, then, were like, inseparable."

"Paul left The Lasers to stay with Gary," confirmed Annette Gardiner, *"because the other members didn't want to use Gary's material. Paul preferred Gary's song writing so he also decided to leave the band. That's when Gary and Paul went their own way and Jess (Gerald) Lidyard, Gary's uncle, came in on drums. I was really just mates with Paul at the time and Paul never spoke much about the others. Paul was not a big talker unless it was relevant to Tubeway Army."*

"We did just one proper gig before Gary and I decided that we'd go on our own and see what we could do," remembered Paul, *"The Lasers split up soon after we left. I was sure that Gary was my best bet and it proved to be the right decision."*

"I've really got no idea why he had so much faith in me," Gary revealed during a later interview, *"I don't think I was doing anything at that time to make somebody think that I could actually do it."*

CHAPTER 4
TUBEWAY DAZE BEGINS

"Please look around, empty faces that can't ever quite die"

(Lyric taken from 'Zero Bars')

Earlier that year, on 23rd April, Andy Czezowski and his business partners, Susan Carrington and Barry Jones suddenly found themselves forcibly evicted from running The Roxy. Rent for the club had been effectively doubled overnight by the club's landlord, who clearly viewed the emergence of punk as a lucrative and cash-heavy goldmine.

Speaking to *3AM* magazine in 2003, Andy Czezowski recalled the day they were told to leave: *"Basically what happened was that The Roxy became a victim of its own success, the two old queens who owned it saw it making money for the first time in ages and cashed in by selling it. So they sold it and the first I knew about it was when the new owners, some dodgy East End villain types, told me to get out. They booked bands like The Boomtown Rats and the place collapsed, they didn't have a clue or any love for the music, they were just trying to buy into something they saw as successful."*

Undeterred by this setback, Czezowski approached Crackers Discotheque owner, Terry Draper, and managed to cut a deal with him to host punk shows at his venue, under the name of The Vortex, on Monday nights. (later adding Tuesdays) As a live venue, Crackers was much larger than The Roxy, holding 650 people which was gauged by Czezowski to be the perfect size for any aspiring groups wanting to expand their audience.

On 4th July, 1977, Crackers played host to The Vortex for the very first time with the debut live event coming from The Buzzcocks, The Fall and punk poet John Cooper Clarke. A surprise last minute addition to the bill came from Johnny Thunders and the Heartbreakers, who were putting in a final appearance in the UK themselves, before flying back to the US.

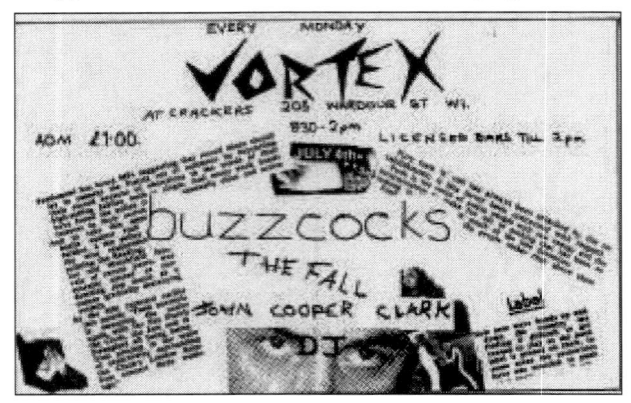

Tubeway Army was also one of the first bands to perform at the Vortex. For Gary though, performing live was to be the cause of so much angst for him on a personal level.

Speaking to *BBC6 Music* in 2015, Gary vividly recalled his early fears when he first stepped in front of an audience. *"I used to be terrified, I came close to being physically sick before every gig we did, before the success came along. I was doing tiny little gigs in pubs to 20 or 30 people and couldn't even talk for two to three days beforehand, I was so nervous, so frightened. It was my Dad who told me 'If you don't find a way of getting around that, then this is the most stupid profession you could have ever tried to get into.' I thought many, many times that I'd chosen the wrong career. I just didn't seem to have the right nature for showmanship."*

For Gary, being periodically surrounded by the simmering violence of a volatile punk crowd was yet another unwelcome strain that did little to placate his inherent nervousness. *"I was playing to an audience which was far from converted and was extremely violent,"* recalled Numan in a later interview, *"and which was about two inches away from my face. I absolutely hated it."*

Despite these less than ideal conditions, Gary and Paul would often make their way through the crowds before and after the shows, regularly selling merchandise including t-shirts with the band's name emblazoned in glitter across the front.

They continued their sporadic gig schedule throughout the late summer, appearing once again as a support act on 10th & 15th September, both times at The Roxy. As usual, the DJs, Don Letts and Jerry Floyd provided a welcome relief from the fury of punk by spinning dub reggae between sets.

THE ROXY CLUB 41/43 Neal Street, Covent Garden, WC2

Open 8.30 pm to 2 am

SEPTEMBER
- Tuesday 13th: **Monitones** + Proof — Audition Night
- Wednesday 14th: **The Blanks** + The Look — Audition Night
- Thursday 15th: **Unwanted** + Tube Way Army
- Friday 16th: **Eater** + Dole Q
- Saturday 17th: **Bazoomies** + Nipple Erectors

The Roxy Club

Wednesday September 14th, Audition night adm. 50p
THE BLANKS + THE ROOK

Thursday September 15th
THE UNWANTED + TUBALA ARMY

Friday September 16th
EATER + DOLE QUEUE

Saturday September 17th
BAZOOMIES + NIPPLE ERECTUS

On a couple of occasions during Tubeway Army's performances, and just to break up the set a little, Gary's younger brother John was invited to come up on stage and sing a song himself.

"*John wrote a song, or I should say he wrote the lyrics to a song called 'Lucky' and I stuck some music to it,*" revealed Gary in 1987, "*but I only put the same music to it the way that he actually sang it. I just played along to it and arranged it for him and he did it.*"

John Webb added: "*Gary and I were at home one day in 1976 or 1977. I was eleven years old at the time. I walked in the front room and I was singing this song 'Lucky' which I'd just thought up. Gary asked 'What's that?' He liked it and grabbed a guitar to put a riff to it. My Mum sprayed my hair silver which I had to wash out the next morning in time for school. I had three or four safety pins, a swastika badge and a t-shirt with Johnny Silver written on it. Then we started doing it at Tubeway Army gigs. I'd be in the audience and then after five or six*

YOU'RE A LUCKY MAN TO BE OUT OF LONDON.
YOU'RE A LUCKY MAN TO BE OUT OF THE SLUMS.
YOU'RE A LUCKY MAN TO BE OUT OF LONDON.
YOU'RE A LUCKY MAN TO BE OUT OF POLITICS
YOU'RE A LUCKY MAN TO BE OUT OF POLITICS
YOU'RE A LUCKY MAN TO BE OUT OF LONDON.
YOU'RE A LUCKY MAN TO BE IN HEAVEN.
YOU'RE A LUCKY MAN TO BE OUT OF LONDON.
YOU'RE A LUCKY MAN TO BE DEAD.
YOU'RE A LUCKY MAN TO BE DEAD

songs I'd jump on stage and start shouting this track. I did this on and off for about a year."

"He always got the biggest cheer of the night," recalled Gary fondly, *"he really did. He used to be on stage for three or four minutes, do his song and then go off again, the crowd used to love him."*

In the meantime, the stagnating British music scene was at last enjoying a welcome influx of new blood into the upper reaches of the pop charts. A neutered and therefore 'acceptable' version of punk rock called 'New Wave' had emerged. This prompted the BBC's flagship chart show, *Top of the Pops* to finally allow some of the less volatile bands making headway in the singles chart, to mix with the insipid 70s pop that padded out the remainder of the roster on the weekly programme.

Electronic music was also beginning to create a presence in the UK pop charts, seeing Donna Summer's epic Giorgio Moroder produced song, 'I Feel Love' monopolising the top spot during the height of the summer. This was followed soon after by a song called 'Magic Fly', a quirky synthetic instrumental, performed by French group, Space.

CHAPTER 5
DEMO DAYS REJECTED

"It's always so close but never quite arrives"
(Lyric from 'Listen to the Sirens')

According to John Savage, in his book *England's Dreaming*, the official date of punk's demise was marked thus, *"the accelerated motion of punk culture and new wave business had reached the point of burnout in London by the autumn of 1977."*

Gary later bolstered this statement when interviewed about the era of late 70s punk, *"Punk had no future to it whatsoever. It was purely fashion, I remember going into a shop and seeing a T-shirt that was burnt and one that wasn't and you paid more for the one that was burnt!"*

When punk culture exploded, kicking and screaming into the psyche of the unsuspecting British public in 1976, there was little doubt that at the very least, it was something new, and so it was welcomed as a fresh and exciting change after decades of mostly safe music output in the UK. It did initially reach out and challenge the established order of things, but as a scene it was to be quickly dispelled.

In late 1976, the Sex Pistols' expletive-laden appearance on ITV's *Bill Grundy Show*, jolted a nation into simultaneous shock and fascination. When interviewed for *England's Dreaming*, journalist John Ingham, then best known for writing the first ever interview with the Sex Pistols for *Sounds* magazine in April 1976, noted the Bill Grundy episode as a pivotal point in the punk movement. This was independently confirmed by Adam And The Antz guitarist Marco Pirroni, both he and Ingham pointing to the Pistols' sloppy TV appearance as the very moment that punk's true meaning was lost. *"A lot of people that had been on the scene disappeared as soon as Grundy happened,"* Ingham recalled, *"it became stupid very quickly and no-one with any snazz wanted to be associated with anything like that."* Marco Pirroni agreed. *"Bill Grundy was the end of it for me, from something artistic and almost intellectual in weird clothes, suddenly there were these fools with dog*

collars on and 'punk' written on their shirts in biro."

Despite his reservations over the band's musical direction, Gary pressed on, with Tubeway Army performing as support to Penetration at The Roxy on 1st October. Although Gary instinctively realised that punk was nothing more than a passing fad, frustratingly, he still had no clear idea of exactly where he should take his own musical direction. A flicker of what was to change his life in such an enormous way, occurred on 9th October when Gary and long-time friend Nick Robson went to an Ultravox! concert at London's Roundhouse. This event was just a week before the band was booked to record its first demo tape in a professional sound recording studio.

Ultravox! had been carefully and painstakingly assembled in the mid-70s by its leader and vocalist, John Foxx, and at this juncture the band had just released its second studio album, *Ha!-Ha!-Ha!* This latest offering ditched the relentless power-chording and instead throbbed with the sounds of synthesisers and drum machines.

During his contribution to a radio documentary in 2010, *Totally Wired: Artists in Electronic Sound*, Foxx recalled his musical vision for a new kind of group as the 1980s dawned. *"I decided to design a band that incorporated Englishness but looked over to Europe, rather than America, for influences and ideas. Also, I wanted to pursue a tradition of electronic music that started with the Beatles that had never been exploited after they broke up. I think 'Strawberry Fields Forever' was one of the first electronic records ever that was popular in England. And it was electronic; there were acoustic instruments on it, but everything was heavily treated and reorganized via tape. I remember that record as being one of the most exciting things, in fact one of the first things that affected me musically. Then a few things happened like Roxy Music that I thought was very exciting. And Kraftwerk were the first people who had isolated all the elements of pop music and synthesized them; they were using no acoustic instruments, or very few."*

Having earned enough money to buy some new equipment, the members of Ultravox! purchased their first synthesisers, notably an ARP Odyssey and a Roland TR77 drum machine, both of which were used on the track 'Hiroshima Mon Amour'. This song, more than any other, exemplified what would become the group's subsequent synth-pop direction. In contrast to Kraftwerk's cold, clinical and somewhat Germanic use of synthesised sound, Ultravox!'s recordings were more organic and there was a warmth and a humanness to their electronic endeavours. In fact, such has been the impact since the release of 'Hiroshima Mon Amour' that according to the website *Quiet City*: "The world can be divided into two kinds of people: those who have heard 'Hiroshima Mon Amour', and those who haven't."

"I think no one else had done a song like that before," recalled Foxx when speaking to *Peek-A-Boo* magazine, *"nobody had used the drum machine. We tried it as a rock song as well but it was better with a drum machine."*

In the aftermath of the band's Marquee show in the autumn of 1977, journalist Chas de Whalley, writing for the *New Musical Express*, heaped some welcome and long overdue praise on the band, *"Ultravox! have come in for their share of criticism since Island Records launched them with a bang eight months ago"* he wrote, *" but if their Marquee appearance was anything to go by, Ultravox! are finally 'getting it all together'. In places Ultravox! were almost awe-inspiring."*

Whether seeing this performance of Ultravox! had any notable influence on Gary is unclear, and certainly outwardly there was nothing to indicate a sea change in his approach with Tubeway Army. The group continued to persevere with an unconvincing punk rock stance, though in later interviews Gary revealed the inner workings of his mind during this period and also the vague plan he had in place when speaking with Peter Gilbert in 1987.

"I used punk solely as a means of getting a contract, I didn't see it going anywhere. I don't think it has gone anywhere. I always saw it as a movement, especially in the early days before it became fashionable. I was excited by the thing as a whole, that all of a sudden there was a completely new fashion, new music. I thought the punk thing was terrible though. People were spitting, being sick and all kinds of revolting things. The punk thing was just so down, anti-hero, vicious and unpleasant in general. It shook the music business up sure, but it wasn't particularly good musically, or visually very good. All those punk bands looked so boring, there wasn't an interesting individual amongst them; they weren't the answer to what people were looking for. I knew that the punk sound couldn't last, it was dying on its feet but people were too frightened to admit it."

"About three months after I met Paul," recalled Annette Louise Gardiner, *"I split up with my boyfriend and I was on my own. I didn't have many friends and I was working in a hairdresser's before I worked for EMI. Initially Paul and I were just mates but later when we were an item, we'd go out to watch live bands in London. I was introduced to punk as well as the Velvets, Iggy Pop, and Ultravox! but I was into disco before I met Paul and had never even heard of Lou Reed! Paul*

introduced me to the deeper side of music. I was a disco girl, I grew up with Frank Sinatra, The Rolling Stones and The Beatles, although I did like Marc Bolan and The Monkees when I was a kid. But I liked what Paul played me anyway, it was one of the reasons why we had lot in common. On one weekend trip when we'd gone to see live bands, Paul and I went to a venue called The Rock Garden in Covent Garden. This was in October 1977, and I remember it being cold because I wore a tweed coat to keep me warm. Paul was meeting someone called Gary. I didn't really meet Gary properly that evening as he seemed to be in a rush. Paul said Gary was checking out some of the competition, some of the other bands."

So Tubeway Army's next move was to record a demo tape, the only accepted method for any band to get through the doors of potential record companies.

"My first 'proper' recording session was in a place called Spaceward in Cambridge," enthused Gary to Peter Gilbert in 1988, *"where I learned an awful lot from the people there. Mike Kemp, in particular, was great. He was pretty sick to death of punk bands falling in and falling out, because that was the cheapest music industry in the country at that time. The sixteen-track studios were mainly home-built, and my Dad paid for the recording sessions. To me it was great. I even used to put on my special clothes to go there. It was an event for me. It was a very special event. I've always felt that you often feel the way you dress, which is why I'm probably so image conscious. I've always found that that was important, so thought I ought to go into the studio looking a certain way, to help create the atmosphere of what I was going to be doing."*

Spaceward Studios, according to Stephen Roper's book *Back Stage,* was a hugely popular 16-track recording facility which was comprised of two terraced houses in Cambridge that had been knocked together to form the studio complex. Most of the rooms were rented out to the musicians who used the facility, and all recordings took place in the basement studio. Spaceward's popularity with local bands was mainly due to its affordable prices and its easy accessibility from central London.

For the upcoming recording session, Gary asked his uncle Gerald to play drums, even though Gerald had previously made it clear to Gary that the punk scene definitely wasn't for him, apparently quoting Elton John's now classic comment, *"punk sounded like a lot of semi-pros just having a bash."*

"I didn't have a permanent drummer during this time so my uncle Gerald came in. We had gigs up and coming so Gerald filled in for us until we could get another drummer in, which we did. Gerald didn't fit in

at first; he was very flash trying to impress us how good he was all the time."

In total, the band demoed three tracks: 'That's Too Bad', 'Oh! Didn't I Say' and 'Out Of Sight', all recorded consecutively on Sunday, 16th October. 'That's Too Bad' was positioned as the lead track as it was clearly the most commercial of the three, with Gary later commenting, *"The song was written 99% to get a contract; it was a naive attempt to make a punk commercial, which it didn't do."*

But it was during this recording session at Spaceward that Gerald noticed a distinct change in Gary, a noticeable strengthening of his character. He later explained, *"From that first session at Spaceward when we did 'That's Too Bad', Gary gradually got to be more assertive. He had a silent battle of wits with the man at the control desk who tried to impose his technical ideas on Gary. By the time we returned to make a complete album, Gary was telling the guy in the studio just what he wanted. He quickly earned his respect."*

But now, with a demo tape in their possession, Gary and Paul had to begin the arduous and seemingly pointless process of trying to find someone connected to the music business who would listen to it. This at a time when The Sex Pistols were controversially topping the album charts with their debut album, *Never Mind The Bollocks* and there was an avalanche of punk fanzines like Mark Perry's *Sniffin' Glue* clogging up the magazine racks. So trying to get someone to listen to the demo tape was clearly going to be much harder than any of them could have imagined.

"We took a cassette around to everybody we could think of except for the really big record companies because I found them too intimidating." Gary later recalled, *"You had the big glass doors and grand entrance and the snotty receptionist who had an attitude that you couldn't believe and I thought I can't deal with any of that. The punk thing was really going so we went to all the little punk labels where we thought we might get a slightly friendlier reception and they were just as evil, nasty. I was nineteen and it crushed me. We tried for a long time; we went running after label after label after label. I did it initially myself and then I just lost heart. But Paul carried on going. During the very early days of Tubeway Army, Paul was the one going out trying to sell us but they just kept turning us down all over the place."*

Although Gary was justified in feeling disheartened with the complete lack of response from the record labels, Paul didn't share that same emotion. He just dug his heels in, relentless in his efforts for the band, banging on any door he could find. Paul's confidence in Gary's talent was more than enough to spur him on. But despite all of their combined efforts, record company interest in Tubeway Army proved to be flat-lining, so much so that Gary began to feel that perhaps another batch of songs might be necessary at this point to make a completely different impact with the music executives. Until a chance encounter one day, in Ealing.

CHAPTER 6
BEGGARS BANQUET RECORDS

"I've waited thousands of years for this prize"
(Lyric from 'Crime Of Passion')

"Paul and I had just about given up on getting a deal and we were about to record another demo when Paul walked into the Beggars Banquet shop to sell some second-hand records one day and was talking to the bloke behind the desk and he mentioned that he was in a band. He also mentioned that we had a tape and the bloke said that the people who owned the shop had just started up their own little label and he said 'give it to me and I'll pass it on.' He went up to Earls Court and passed it onto Martin Mills and Nick Austin. The one in Fulham had a rental place in the basement for rehearsals, the one Paul went to in Ealing was where Steve Webbon worked."

Paul's dogged persistence seemed as though it had finally paid off which came as a huge relief at that time. When he was asked to revisit this time period during a later interview, he explained, *"As Gary joined my band, The Lasers, I felt like I was still responsible in a way, to make sure the new group got somewhere. So I did most of the talking when I went to Beggars Banquet."*

"Paul was definitely the talkative one of the two," remembered label boss Martin Mills, *"which surprises me now because later we were all able to see how he was, underneath, more shy than Gary. It's quite amazing now to reflect on how quiet Gary was on that first meeting and in the very early days. He just followed Paul around and seemed content to chip in the odd sentence but Paul kept on impressing us with his terrific enthusiasm and stories of how good the band was going to be, how it was not just another punk band, and how good the tape would be and would we listen to it quickly!"*

Beggars Banquet Records had started life as a mobile disco in London during the early 1970s under the arty progressive name Giant Elf. Over time, Giant Elf was eventually replaced by the much more palatable name of Beggars Banquet. In 1973 Martin and his business partner Nick Austin opened up their first record shop in Earls Court with more stores following soon after. By 1976, many of the local punk bands in the area began to use the basement underneath the Fulham shop for rehearsals for upcoming gigs.

"One of the bands that used to rehearse down there was The Lurkers," recalled Mills, *"and the shop manager (Mike Stone) started to manage them. He needed help so we started managing them. We tried to*

get them a record deal but nobody wanted them because at that point, everyone had already signed a punk band. So we did what seems really normal these days, because the road map is really well travelled now, but in those days it was almost unprecedented, we put the record out ourselves ('Free Admission' in August 1977). We pressed it and got a very old-fashioned distributor called President to take it on."

Peter Haynes, drummer with The Lurkers, concurred: *"Beggars Banquet Records was formed because of The Lurkers, we used to rehearse in Fulham and it was the beginning of the punk days."*

Eventually Gary and Paul, along with their newly acquired drummer Bob Simmonds, were asked to play a rehearsal in the basement of the Fulham shop.

"My involvement in punk began when I was 19," recalled Bob, *"I answered an ad in the music magazine Melody Maker asking for a drummer, I ended up in Tubeway Army when they were then going through their early punk phase. I signed on the dole and moved to London, living on friends' floors in Earls Court and Soho."*

After the rehearsal, Martin, Nick and Steve, having been impressed by what they'd heard and seen, thought it would be a good idea to see the band in a proper live setting if they had any intention to sign Tubeway Army to the label.

On 6th December the band were due to support Merger, Rage and Bazoomies at the Vortex. It is assumed that this is the show that Mills, Austin and Webbon first saw Tubeway Army live.

Tuesday, December 6th
"Roots Reggae Rockers"
MERGER
The Rage The Bazoomies Tubeway Army

Martin Mills: *"When the band played the Vortex, Gary was just incredible up there on that stage. He seemed incredibly nervous beforehand but the way he looked at the audience, the confidence, the way he held the microphone, just everything about him was magnetic. He had blonde hair, his look really had something and he handled the audience just brilliantly."*

Mills and the rest of the label were not to know that Gary's onstage confidence was merely an act, masking the severe stage fright from which he regularly suffered. However, this single live performance at the Vortex proved to Martin and Beggars Banquet that Tubeway Army was indeed an act worth signing.

"It was when they saw us live, or saw me on stage, that they decided to sign us up," remembered Gary fondly, "and apparently they saw something about the way I was on stage that they liked. They said I had a command of the audience, which is ridiculous because there were only about three people there!"

Beggars eventually agreed to a trial single and promised the group some regular live work though Gary felt the real reason for their interest was the fact that the band had arrived at their doorstep prepped and ready.

"I believe that the only reason Beggars took us on is because my Dad had bought us a van and a PA system and we had our own gear. And we'd already recorded the songs. They didn't have to do it. So they had to put out virtually no money. They saw what I had done with the 'That's Too Bad' single as being punk made commercial. Not quite so 'anti' in the lyric, and the fact that we could play helped enormously, one of the first punk bands that actually played properly. We weren't great musicians but at least we could play in tune and we knew what a note was. To be fair to them, they said that they couldn't afford to take on another band at that time which I know from my own experience, a new label is actually stretched financially to promote new bands because they only take so many. And so because we had all this gear, they took us on, again thanks entirely to my Dad who had now spent his life savings on this equipment, which is unbelievable really when you think of it. Just a working class bloke who spent about twenty odd years of his life working to get this little bit of money and then only because his son wants to be famous. I don't think my Dad really felt in his heart of hearts that I would make it as a big success."

Peter Haynes: *"I have to say Beggars Banquet weren't very receptive to Gary in the beginning. When he wanted to get a record done they said that they'd only do the distribution; I think that this was because they didn't really have the confidence in him. I remember Gary's dad was a haulier or something and he had a bit of money saved up so it was actually Gary's family that did much of the work, getting Gary to a studio, paying for the session etc because Beggars Banquet, in all their wisdom, didn't think he was going to do much. As it transpired he went on to make them millionaires. It wasn't a case of them creating him, it was a case of Gary creating himself."*

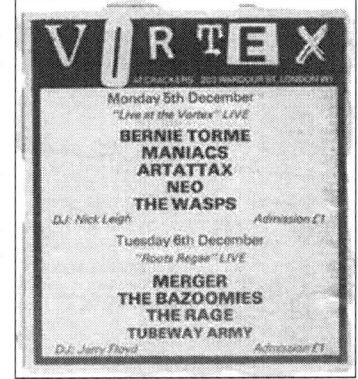

VORTEX

Monday 5th December
"Live at the Vortex" LIVE
BERNIE TORME
MANIACS
ARTATTAX
NEO
THE WASPS
DJ: Nick Leigh   Admission £1

Tuesday 6th December
"Roots Reggae" LIVE
MERGER
THE BAZOOMIES
THE RAGE
TUBEWAY ARMY
DJ: Jerry Floyd   Admission £1

For Gary though, just to sign a record deal was everything he'd ever wanted. *"I was a little spotty punk rocker and was just glad to be signed by a label. Not long after, I remember we supported Adam And The Antz at The Roxy."*

Unfortunately, exact details about this support slot still remain a mystery but research seems to point to one possible date on 16th December where Adam And The Antz shared the Roxy stage with three other support acts, The Red Lights, The Tax Exiles as well as Billy Karloff & The Goats. In addition, three shows that took place in January 1978 may also have been the support slot that Gary was referring to, those being the gigs on 7th January (Adam & The Ants, Blitz, The Purge). 21st January (Adam & The Ants, Richard III, Plastix) and 28th January (Adam & The Ants, Virus, Perverse Velvet).

With the Beggars Banquet roster of artists growing monthly, an increase in income for the record label was beginning to become a much more serious aspect of the business as 1977 drew to a close. So much so that it became necessary for Beggars to open additional stores to increase turnover to fund the label. Grateful though to finally have a record contract and to be seen to be supporting the company, Paul and Gary would often offer their time when asked to help out around the various Beggars Banquet shops, as Gary explained to Peter Gilbert in a later interview.

"The main shop was in Earls Court. In fact I helped build another in Richmond. I had to go in and help them put up shelves when I wasn't famous so I thought it was a way to get signed. It was like a little family. It was great. Me and Paul used to trot out and go and build a shop. I don't know if it's still there but if anyone goes out to that shop in Richmond, I built it."

"None of us were getting much money for doing gigs then - about £5 a night," revealed the bands sound man Peter Edwards, *"so when Beggars opened a new shop in Richmond they paid Gary myself and a couple of other people to refurbish it."*

Following the bands final live appearance of the year on 12th December (supporting the Satellites along with another band called The Cioaca) at the Oriel Youth Centre in Northolt Gary, Paul and Bob took a welcome break as the holidays approached.

On 23rd December, Beggars sent the band's demo multitrack to Manor Studios in Oxford asking for 'That's Too Bad' to be remixed for a more commercial sound. The label had decided that this was the most obvious choice as a first single from the band. The main area of interest for Beggars, was Gary's vocal which the label wanted to move further forward in the mix because they felt that he was too far back in the demo version. Mick Glossop was the assigned engineer that day at Manor

Studios and this is what he said to author Howard Massey in 2000 about the methods he used then and still uses today when presented with raw demos.

"When I first listen to demos of a band, they'll give me an idea of what their direction is. From the demos, I'll form an idea of where I think I need to make changes musically and sonically, but also I start to get an idea of how I think the record could sound, but not too specifically at that point. Then I meet the band. We talk about the sound, the sort of things they like, the sort of records they want to make, and that sort of crystallizes that idea of what sort of sound the record's going to have. That's the reference for virtually all the decisions that are made, notwithstanding the fact that you are going to have some experimentation and some surprises along the way."

When the new mix was delivered back to the label, Martin, Nick and Steve were delighted with the results and set the wheels in motion to release the song as Tubeway Army's debut single in the New Year.

1978

CHAPTER 7
THE TOURING PRINCIPLE

"I've no time for the chitter chatter ladies, I'm so busy trying to break this wall"

(Lyric taken from 'Friends')

With the band's debut single 'That's Too Bad' scheduled for release in early February, Beggars Banquet hastily added Tubeway Army as support act for The Lurkers in the hope of generating some much needed attention for the band.

"The record company said that they had an act to support us and it was Tubeway Army fronted by Gary," recalled Lurkers drummer Peter Haynes, *"although he was a local lad he came from the other side of the airport and we were from out west. We toured with Tubeway Army on and off for months and we did quite a few gigs with them as I recall. You have to remember that we weren't playing football stadiums; we were playing these punk clubs and Tubeway Army were our support band. They weren't ever bottled off but the audiences were definitely a bit rowdy. After we'd gone on, the clubs would clean up and play all the Bowie kind of stuff for the rest of the evening and people really liked that kind of music because it was just so different to the punk scene."*

On 28th January, Tubeway Army performed their first show of the year at The Rochester Castle pub in Stoke Newington, and again a week later on 4th February at Dingwalls, this time behind two additional Beggars Banquet acts, The Dolls and Johnny G. Following the latter show, an unexpected review appeared in the music press written by Mick Wall of *Sounds* magazine, singling out Gary and his band for high, if slightly inappropriate praise.

"Tubeway Army began the festivities and at once succeeded in making a favourable impression. They're a threesome from the London vicinity all aged just 17 and they play some pretty damn good rock and roll, this being one of their first gigs. It's the potential you have to look for rather than the finished article. Kudos everywhere to them for turning in such a promising debut. In Valeriun (vocals, guitar) they have going for them what undoubtedly is their strongest visual asset. Blond-haired, blue-eyed visage that promises to dampen the knickers of many a sweet young thing once given the right kind of exposure."

One of the most noticeable things that set Gary apart from many of his peers during this period was his strong family base at home. Whereas most punk musicians distanced themselves from their parents, Gary actively encouraged his mother Beryl and his father Tony as well as younger brother John to join him as he slogged around the various punk venues during the band's early days.

"We were all very impressed that a musician's father was carrying their equipment," recalled Martin Mills when speaking to Ray Coleman in 1982, *"everybody from Beggars Banquet and the people in the clubs were surprised that somebody's father would not only drive them around and listen to the music but physically help their son's band setting up the gear."*

"My family moved into the next street to where Gary lived in 1966 or 67 I think, when I was around five or six years old," recalled Nick Robson, *"Gary's Mum and Dad, Beryl and Tony, were kind of like the ultimate parents to all of us, I guess. We'd spend the day playing football or watching TV or just hanging out on the street corner and as kids, we were in a perpetual state of hunger but Beryl was always there to feed you, she'd never let you go hungry so all I have are the fondest memories of growing up around them during my entire childhood. Just extraordinarily wonderful people. Gary's uncle, Jess, used to leave his Rickenbacker electric guitar for Gary to use and it was the first guitar I'd ever touched and I hoped that somehow I might own one of my own some day."*

"Gary's Dad was always around," recalled Peter Haynes, "after the gig he'd be there getting the gear into the back of the transit van. Tony was always pleasant to me and he'd often buy me a pint."

It's during this flurry of live work that Gary began to further examine the visual aspect and presentation of not only the band as a whole but also the way in which he wanted to project his own image within it, something picked up on by the young singer's good friend Garry Robson, *"The band didn't look particularly different in jeans and t-shirts and they were always fairly stationary on stage. It was one of the things that was not very punk about them because they didn't pogo or jump around. Tubeway Army weren't really punk; it was variations on the sort of things we'd grown up with, T.Rex, Bowie and Lou Reed but very much more based on guitar, bass and drums at that time."*

When interviewed for the 2015 book *Love In Vain - The Story Of The Ruts*, drummer David Ruffy humorously recalled his first encounter with the members of Tubeway Army when his band, along with support act, Misty In Roots, were due to headline a show in Hayes on 2nd June 1978. *"They were all leather clad and Goth looking, slightly military: if you imagine punk meets Planet Of The Apes."*

With the band picking up good press and gradually gaining a small but dedicated following, Beggars decided to put the group on a retainer. The £15 a week Gary received enabled him to finally quit his day job and concentrate on the band full time.

"I worked for a company called W.H. Smith, the book company," Gary remembered when talking to Peter Gilbert in 1986, *"I worked there until the day my first single came out on the 10th of February."*

Just prior to the single's release, Gary, Paul and Bob attended a photo session posing for a series of shots for the record's picture sleeve. In an attempt to set the band apart from the safety pins and ripped clothing of the punk hordes, Gary presented the band as a futuristic, science fiction themed act complete with spacey costumes and stage names. So Bob, Paul and Gary became Rael, Scarlett and Valeriun respectively. According to long time friend Nick Robson, Valeriun may have been adapted from the name of the prescription tranquilizers that Gary had been taking during his time at college.

"I wanted to be mysterious and spacey," explained Numan much later, *"It was an incredibly embarrassing attempt by me to sound futuristic which seemed important at the time. It just made me look like an idiot really. It was a notable mistake."*

A cursory examination of the lyrics to 'That's Too Bad' revealed a songwriter with a strong interest in science fiction.

"I was into sci-fi, I was writing collections of songs where, lyrically, they would all fit together. There was one called 'Warriors of Marnz' that was part of a whole collection of stuff built around sci-fi."

Unfortunately, the costumes that had been used for the record sleeve photo session, became a problem when the band performed live, particularly Gary's suit.

"I wore the 'spacesuit' on the back of the sleeve of the 'That's Too Bad' single once at a gig at Ashford Grammar School in Middlesex. It wasn't a spacesuit exactly, it was a little two piece number bought from Kings Road I might add, made out of some high tech insulating material so it was f*cking hot!"

"Gary was an individualist" remembers Peter Haynes, *"and he'd turn up for a photo session dressed up like someone from Star Trek or something, very futuristic."*

Despite this short-lived and dubious image, the band's debut single was released on schedule on 10th February costing just 69p in the shops, and encouragingly for the band and the label, the single immediately began to generate sales.

"'That's Too Bad' sold out 4,000 copies quite rapidly," recalled Mills, *"but we got no radio play with the record. Those were the days when there were so few punk/new wave records coming out on small labels that people following that sound would buy anything that was remotely punk or on a small label. They'd buy them almost without knowing whether they liked them or not. I loved 'That's Too Bad'. I actually thought it was really, really good."*

With a debut 7-inch single out in the shops and selling, Tubeway Army continued to tour with label-mates The Lurkers, supporting them on 19th February at The Marquee Club, The Rock Garden on the 21st, The Cambridge Corn Exchange on the 24th (this time as support to The Adverts) with the last show of the month taking place at the Royal Hotel in Luton, a gig that turned out to be particularly violent.

Suddenly thrust into a regularly gigging band, new drummer Bob revealed in a later interview, the environment that he, Gary and Paul had to endure, *"There was so much spitting going on at the gigs that you'd end up drenched in saliva but being spat on by punk fans was a sign that they liked you. It was seen as a compliment! Back then the music was so loud you couldn't hear for three days afterwards. We played at an*

amazing speed so I was quite fit. There was something ritualistic about a punk gig with everyone crammed in. There was a real sense of community. In those days no one had anything so we shared what we did have."

Frustratingly for fans of this early version of Tubeway Army, only one live recording has since been discovered, although it's understood that subsequent shows were taped from this period and may still exist. As a consequence, it's impossible to accurately track the evolution of the band's live set over the course of its existence, though it's clear from later interviews that the band's roster of songs was changing and updating quite rapidly.

"The set was constantly changing," remembered Beggars Banquet art director Steve Webbon, *"I got the impression that Gary was reading a lot at the time. He'd have a riff for a song and some basic lyrics and sometimes they'd play it live. Then he'd go back, re-write it and change the title."*

Nick Robson added, *"At this point in my own career, I was working in Wardour Street in Soho, so whenever Gary was playing at a London venue, I found it easy to go and watch the band and help out with the gear. In a fairly short space of time, I realised that I knew all the lyrics to the songs in the set but I didn't have a clue what the songs were called. I just loved the raw power at these gigs and Gary possessed a very distinct and unique charisma that was clear to me and to the audience at that time. It was like watching something new about to be born."*

For Gary though, renewing and reinventing the set list was just his way of keeping things fresh. *"Punk songs were so easy,"* he later explained, *"you just churned them out. One night I decided three or four of the songs we'd been using were a bit tired. So I wrote three new ones the next morning. We rehearsed them in the afternoon and performed them in the evening. I found writing easy in those days because it didn't matter so much if I repeated myself."*

But the band's sole surviving live document, a performance recorded at The Rock Garden on 21st February, provides a unique time capsule with Gary, Paul and Bob blasting through the following twelve songs: 'Positive Thinking', 'Blue Eyes', 'My Shadow In Vain', 'That's Too Bad', 'Basic J', 'Do Your Best', 'Oh! Didn't I Say', 'Me, My Head', 'Boys', 'You Don't Know Me', 'I'm A Poseur' and finally 'Kill St Joy'. (A 13th track, 'White Light/White Heat', a cover of the classic Velvet Underground song, has also emerged, though this recording is understood to have been taken from an earlier show in November, 1977 when the band supported Penetration at The Roxy)

However, it is fair to say that listening to this lone recording today, a lot of the songs featured are fairly crude examples of Tubeway Army simply churning out punk by numbers for the attendant punk crowd, with some of them seeming like relatively meaningless tunes devoid of any real soul or content, as Gary confirmed," *In truth, on many of these songs, I used to make them up as I went along, whenever we played live. Nobody could understand a word you were singing anyway and the PA systems were so awful so it didn't seem to matter. It was the attitude that carried the message, if you had a message, and I didn't even have that half the time. The lyrics to the early punky songs - I haven't the remotest idea what any of the words are.*"

Unlike the simmering anger found in punk lyrics, Gary's writing relied more on a cocktail of literary illusions, personal isolation, paranoia and teenage loneliness. Real life situations were also gradually beginning to filter into his song writing. Two songs in particular, 'Positive Thinking' and 'Kill St Joy', were both written in the aftermath of two separate and wholly unpleasant incidents.

"*'Kill St Joy' was named after the owner of The Roxy Club,*" revealed Numan to Peter Gilbert in 1987, "*a man called Kevin St John. I remember one night when I was 19 or 20, I was locked in a room with a huge gangster who wanted to f**k me up the arse because he thought I would do anything to play in his club. That scared the shit out of me! I didn't want the gig that badly!*"

And as for 'Positive Thinking', this song owes its genesis to a relatively amusing situation that Paul, Gary and his father Tony experienced, following a gig at a local scout hut. The trio had visited a potential manager for the band at his home address only to discover that he was in fact nothing more than a spaced-out and self-appointed Guru surrounded by wasted drug addicts.

"*It was like something out of a Beatles film,*" recalled Gary to Steve Malins in 1997, "*but on a housing estate in Hayes. I wrote the song as a reminder to Paul about the dangers of listening to idiots. He took it well and we laughed about it for years afterward.*"

Of the twelve songs performed at The Rock Garden, six were never recorded as studio versions by the band. Of those, 'Kill St Joy', 'You Don't Know Me' and 'Positive Thinking' are easily the best with all three bristling with the band's belligerent and strutting punk rock energy, which seems lacking in the other three tracks, 'Boys', 'I'm A Poseur' and 'Me, My Head'. Happily though, this rare live document, itself once available as a live vinyl bootleg in the early 80s, can now be found tagged onto the end of the 1998 CD reissue of the self-titled Tubeway Army album.

CHAPTER 8
DISCOVERY

"This machine is my voice, please listen"
(Lyric taken from 'This Machine')

With Tubeway Army now regularly performing live, it quickly became apparent that the band had certain physical limitations as a live act. After reviewing the feedback from the gigs, Martin Mills came up with what he felt was a solution that would help the band overcome the stumbling blocks they were experiencing. *"At Beggars,"* Mills reasoned, *"we all felt that another guitarist was necessary in Tubeway Army because Gary felt restricted. He had to sing, move around the stage, play guitar and write."*

However, when the idea was suggested to Gary, he felt sure there was a very different reason as to why the label felt the need for a second guitarist. *"Beggars Banquet always wanted me to start duo guitar things, like one guitar doing one part and another guitar doing another. Possibly more musical but not what I intended the other guitar to be for. But that's what Sean Burke was possibly in for - to be that other guitarist. I didn't want to have a band with two guitars in it where two guitars were doing different things. I simply wanted to make what I was playing on the guitar more powerful. So I wanted another guitar to be doing exactly the same thing. I wanted both guitars to be doing the same thing to create a very powerful sound. But Martin never quite understood what I was after."*

But not wanting to damage the reasonably harmonious relationship between the label and the band, Gary accepted Martin's suggestion and an ad was placed in the music press, eventually attracting the attention of local guitarist, Sean Burke. He recalled,*" A friend of mine came round to see me one day to tell me there was a band in the Melody Maker called Tubeway Army and they needed a guitarist and that they had a record deal. I remember saying 'oh, that's not me, that's professional stuff.'"*

Although Sean was initially hesitant to call the number in the ad, he wasn't exactly inexperienced, musically. He had already been in two bands, the first, a progressive act called Paradox and the second, a short-lived punk band called Open Sore.

"At the end of that particular day I rang them," continued Sean, *"and spoke to Gary's Dad (Tony Webb) and he basically said to me that they'd closed the auditions. So I said 'oh, that's a shame.' He then asked me where I lived and at that time I lived in small town in Aylesbury. Tony said if I could come round at 7.30 then they'd see me first. At the time it was 6 o'clock. Anyway I got there and it was Paul Gardiner, Gary and a guy called Bob Simmonds, and Bob held the audition at his parent's house. We did 'Waiting For The Man,' 'White Light White Heat' and I think we did 'Blue Eyes' and 'That's Too Bad.' We all seemed to be getting on and then Gary went upstairs for some reason and Paul said to me 'I think you've got it.' I asked him, 'Why, I mean you've got about 45 people to see yet?' and Paul said 'No, I know him; I think you've got the gig.' I just said 'OK, whatever, I'm going out now' and off I went."*

Not long after the audition though, Sean received the welcome news that he'd got the nod from Gary, Paul and Bob and that he was now a fully fledged member of Tubeway Army.

Although Gary may have felt uncomfortable about having to bend to the whims of his label, his desire to make the band's sound more powerful was at least now coming to fruition, something that didn't go unnoticed by the group's new guitarist. *"When I auditioned for Tubeway Army, Paul and I found out that we were both into The Velvet Underground and then Tubeway Army started playing 'White Light, White Heat' in the set which sounded great with two guitars, really powerful. Gary and I both had the same HH 1C100 amplifier and the same guitar, a Les Paul deluxe which has a powerful sound as did these amps."*

However, road-testing the group's new line-up was the next big hurdle and an unexpected problem came up just prior to their next scheduled gig when drummer, Bob Simmonds, suddenly gave his notice to leave. Sean takes up the story. *"I rehearsed for the first time with the band in a hall in West Drayton for, I think, something like two weeks before I had my first gig with Tubeway Army. I remember we went to this place for an afternoon rehearsal and Gary said to me 'I've got bad news, Bob's left the group.' Bob had actually told him on the morning of the gig and obviously this was pretty short notice. So I said 'So we've got no drummer?' and he said 'Don't worry, my uncle's going to do the gig.' So my first gig with the band was with Jess Lidyard."*

"We had gigs up and coming," Gary confirmed in a later interview, *"so Gerald filled in for us until we could get another drummer in. Whenever I didn't have a drummer, Gerald would come in."*

For Bob though, it was the end of the line, not only for his role within the group but the entire punk scene itself. *"I'd had enough of the violence; the gigs were so violent they were bordering on warfare. And I didn't think the band was going anywhere. The record company asked me to rejoin, saying they couldn't find a drummer as good as me but I had had enough. Afterwards I just returned to Basingstoke and went back to the building sites. I left everything from my punk life behind, my clothes, photographs, everything."*

"Neither Beryl or I recall Beggars trying to persuade Bob Simmonds to stay," Gerald recently recalled, *"we think he was pressured by his parents to leave, as well as being uncomfortable at the gigs. Like me, Bob was a pretty average player - that is not to say he was a bad player (like Barry Benn, who would try to play a drum break every four bars, causing problems with producers). But Bob, me and Cedric all sounded similar (Cedric being the best player), so Beggars were pretty relaxed as I was standing in all the time, but I did not want to tour."*

Following a show at The Vortex on 7th March, Gary, Paul and Gerald headed out to Spaceward Studios in Cambridge to begin recording some of the songs the band had been stockpiling. With the band's portfolio of material growing, Gary had previously approached Beggars Banquet, asking for studio time to begin laying down some of the material that Tubeway Army were now regularly performing live. The band's debut single 'That's Too Bad' had sold well in the previous month so Beggars agreed and booked the band into Spaceward Studios. This particular studio was chosen for two reasons. Firstly, it was relatively cheap and inexpensive to record there but also that the studio's residential location enabled the band to work full days and sleep there too, eliminating travel time. The overall plan for Beggars, was to record a wealth of demo material to see if there was any mileage or potential to release a Tubeway Army punk album. But with their new guitarist largely unfamiliar with the band's growing repertoire it was decided to exclude Sean from the sessions at this stage.

"Sean wasn't up to speed with the songs," confirmed Steve Webbon, *"and Gary only wanted a second guitarist for live shows at that point."*

Clearly thrilled to be back in the studio, Gary took full advantage of the situation, particularly as it seemed to be a relatively open-ended arrangement. Much of the time was spent running the band through their live repertoire, including the raunchy, guitar driven tracks like 'Ice', 'Thoughts No 2' (a track that later morphed into 'It Must Have Been Years'), 'This Is My Life', 'Critics', 'Mean Street', 'Do Your Best' and the Buzzcocks-esque rush of 'Basic J'. Bass duties on day one though were handled by Gary himself as Paul mysteriously failed to appear.

At this moment in time, it is vitally important to note something that happened during these sessions, the pivotal moment that would radically change Gary's career.

"As soon as I walked into the control room, there was a Minimoog. I had never seen one before. I just thought it was the coolest looking thing, just fantastic. Apparently, a rental company was going to come pick it up but the man said I could try it out until they came. I just turned it on and pressed a key and it just sounded huge like ten rock guitars playing at once, a massive sound like a huge big bottom bass roar. All I did was press a key and the room shook! And I just thought, 'F--- me! That's the most amazing thing I've ever heard! The power!' It's just lucky whoever had used it before had left it set up on that sound, if they'd left it on a different sound it might have gone 'dooop' like one of those laughable BBC special effects in the 70s and I would have thought synths were a load of shit. It was just luck that it happened to be there, luck that the hire company hadn't collected it yet and luck that it was left set on this amazing sound. I had this thing for the whole day and it was the most amazing experience."

"Another band had left their gear in the studio," confirmed Gerald in a later interview, *"they'd obviously done a previous session and one of the things they'd left behind was this Moog synth and Gary started playing around with it."*

But despite this chance discovery, the task of mastering the synth proved hugely problematic for Gary, mainly due to his complete lack of familiarity with the instrument. Yet he was intrigued and determined enough to overcome this hurdle, finding time to add its unique sound to three new tracks he'd brought to the studio. Those songs were 'This Machine', 'Check it' and 'Bombers', each featuring Gary's embryonic experimentation with synthesizers.

Listening now to the dozen or so tracks recorded in early March of 1978, it is reasonably clear to see that the group were not particularly convincing as a punk act. Even less so when hearing the two ghostly, Bowie-like, acoustic tracks 'The Monday Troop' and 'Crime Of Passion'. Gary's lyrics also set the band apart from the punk rock hordes, his science-fiction imagery and stark alienation replacing the generic sloganeering and angry vitriol still being touted and shouted by the punk bands.

'My Shadow In Vain', though messy and somewhat under-developed at this point, is a perfect example of Gary's troubled early youth, starkly illustrated in his song-writing. *"I wrote that song when I was about 18; in this song, I sing the line 'Here am I more Roche 5 than pain.' When I was younger, school age, I was sent to a psychologist in an attempt to find out why I was 'disturbed' as they put it. They put me on the drugs, Nardil and Valium for about a year. Roche 5 was written on the Valium tablets."*

But overall, these raw and chaotic recordings from Spaceward demonstrated that Tubeway Army was a band struggling with its own identity, the twelve songs recorded veering wildly from energetic guitar-driven pop punk to fairly bleak acoustic affairs. There were exceptions and 'This Machine' as a perfect example, was undeniably a notable recording. Even in its demo form it was a startling piece of music made all the more remarkable because of Gary's embryonic synthetic embellishments. According to long-time friend and celebrated author Steve Malins, the track was effectively Numan's first electronic pop song. *"'This Machine' evokes human life reduced to machine minding,"* recalled Gary when asked about the song's futuristic and sci-fi originated lyrics, *"'Just my steel friend and me, I stand brave by his side, this machine is all I live for' - It makes you think I suppose."*

The band spent a total of three days recording at Spaceward with Lidyard later noting, *"Paul, Gary and I did something like fifteen or sixteen tracks, just bashing through them."* Yet when the tapes were presented to the label, the general consensus between Mills, Austin and Webbon was that the band had outgrown the majority of the recordings and a true album that represented the band was still some way off. However, that was with the exception of a couple of new demos. One of the new songs that Beggars felt had more to offer was 'Bombers' and in late March, Gary returned to Spaceward to do some more work on the song. For this previously unheard session, Gary worked alone and was allowed for the first time to hire a Minimoog which would in a short time help launch his stratospheric rise to fame and the nomination from his peers, as the Godfather of Electronica.

CHAPTER 9
BOMBERS

"Now the light fades out, and I wonder what I'm doing in a room like this"

(Lyric taken from 'Are 'Friends' Electric?')

While Gary continued working independently on the new version of 'Bombers', guitarist Sean Burke offered the group a quick solution to the now vacant drum seat. A close friend of his, Barry Benn, a member of Sean's previous band, Open Sore, was immediately available. *"I said to Gary, 'Oh, I know a drummer' and that's how Barry got into it. When we rehearsed, it was really loud and I thought we were amazing."*

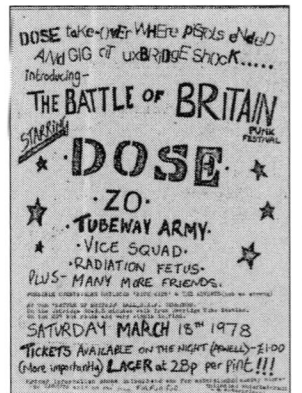

On 18th March, the new and hastily assembled four-man Tubeway Army line-up performed for the first time in Uxbridge, supporting Dos, Zo, Vice Squad and Radiator Foetus. Peter Edwards, the band's soundman during this period, remembered how impressed he was by their enormous amplified sound, *"They had this wall of Les Paul sound which was different to a lot of punk stuff, if anything it reminds me now of Nirvana. I really liked Tubeway Army, they had a good name, they looked good and they made a really good sound."*

At Beggars Banquet, Lurkers manager, Mike Stone, shared Edwards' impression, *"Tubeway Army were a good band although I didn't think of them as punk; there was just something about the sound and look of Tubeway Army that was quite insular and different."*

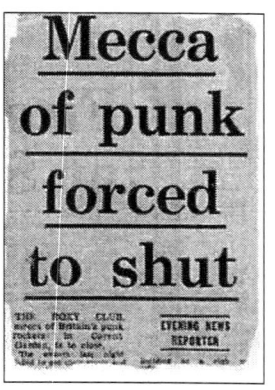

On 3rd April, Tubeway Army played once more at The Vortex. Unbeknownst to the band, this would be their last Vortex performance as the venue was to close its doors for good at the end of that month (with The Roxy following suit just a few weeks later, having finally exhausted its run of appeals and extensions). On 15th April, the group along with Garry Robson, headed off to Wembley to a recording studio called The Music Centre where Tubeway Army were booked to record the new version of 'Bombers'.

"'Bombers' was an important song," recalled Robson, *"because it's the link between Gary's early songs for Beggar's Banquet and the post-punk stuff he did on the Tubeway Army album later in 1978."* For Gary though, the session was important for a very different reason, as it proved to be a significant turning point in his ongoing relationship with Beggars Banquet. *"I wanted Beggars to commit some money because my Dad had paid for the first one and I knew the punk route wasn't what I intended to do. I didn't want to risk losing the contract because I realised they didn't have anything to lose by getting rid of us and as soon as I started giving them stuff that they hadn't signed us for, I knew there would be a temptation on their part to let me go and end the contract. However, once they'd made a financial commitment, they would be more inclined to stick with us and see it through than if they hadn't put any money into us. I don't know if I was right or wrong but that's why I did the 'Bombers' single. They could've said 'No, that's not what we wanted. You'll either do what we want or you'll go.' But it worked."*

During this recording session, Gary was forced to reign in his natural desire for total control due to the fact that Beggars had insisted that the recording be placed under the stewardship and guidance of producer, Kenny Denton.

"I was there when they did the second single, 'Bombers', which has a lot cleaner sound." Garry Robson remembered, *"It was done in a big studio and we lost our way for a while because we were so into the equipment. This was the first time Gary had recorded at a proper studio with lovely EQ and all these effects. So we were having fun with all this stuff and forgot whatever sound we wanted to get at the start of the session."*

"It was an amazing experience to record there," concurred Sean, when speaking online for a radio variety show in 2013, *"it blew my mind."*

Having bankrolled the £1,500 required for the band to record at a professional studio, both Nick Austin and Martin Mills decided they should attend one of the three recording sessions, chipping in ideas along the way. In retrospect, it's true to say that many of these suggestions weren't always welcomed by individual members of the band.

"Beggars originally wanted the song to open with the 'oooohs' on the chorus but we weren't having that." Sean revealed, when later asked about the session. Gary also remembered being forced to alter the song's Bowie-inspired lyrics. *"I remember Nick Austin of Beggars saying 'You*

can't have the line; 'All the junkies with the needles in their arms…' Radio One won't play it.' So I changed it to 'nurses'. So I wasn't really doing what I was told to do but I was sort of listening. I wasn't quite so stubborn."

As well as recording the new version of 'Bombers', the band also found time to lay down demos of two other songs. The older but longtime live favourite, 'Blue Eyes' was recorded along with a brand new track called 'OD Receiver', both of which had been earmarked as B-sides for 'Bombers'. However, reaction to the revised version of 'Bombers' immediately set off alarm bells at Beggars, as Garry Robson later explained, *"When we finished, I think the record company were a bit shocked because 'Bombers' has a much smoother and heavier sound than the punky stuff he'd done before. I think they wanted that homemade, raw sound and that wasn't what we'd delivered."*

A fact Martin Mills later mirrored, *"It was recorded a bit too cleanly for the type of music it was. It ended up as a studio recorded sound, which it isn't in essence. It was smoother than 'That's Too Bad', but not further off in another direction to make it worth going in another direction."*

CHAPTER 10
THE END OF THE LINE

"Something isn't right, I get the feeling I'm not driving, something hasn't quite taken over, but it's trying"
(Lyric taken from 'Check it')

TUBEWAY ARMY
Monday 17th April 1978

For Gary, the joyful high of being in a recording studio was once again sadly short-lived as the grim drudgery of the band's pub-touring experience continued to chip away at him. With the three new tracks recorded and mixed, Tubeway Army immediately returned to live work performing first at Upstairs At Ronnie Scott's on 17th April and then at The Marquee on the 20th, again as support to The Lurkers.

Although Gary's vision for the band and his own musical direction had not yet fully crystallized in his mind, he kept these thoughts to himself for the time being. In May, the band continued their punk assault, playing a trio of shows beginning with The Bones Club in Reading on 1st May (with UK Subs and Dick Envy performing sets in the morning), the Royal Holloway College in Egham and then finally a show in Gary's home town of Wraysbury. In between these performances Gary was also finding time to go and see other bands play, not so much for the music, more for ideas and pointers as to where and where not to take his own career.

"Going to other people's shows was like going to school for me. I would spend as much time looking around the audience as I did looking at the stage. I wanted to find out what was working and what wasn't. What light colour combinations had a good atmosphere and what looked a mess. Did talking to the audience enhance the evening or did it just bore people? You can learn a lot by absorbing the mistakes and triumphs of others."

"I remember once, me and Gary went to see a band called The Depression," recalled Sean, *"and they were about the only punk band*

signed to A&M Records. Anyway we were watching this band down in Kensington and I said to Gary 'good band aren't they?' and he replied 'Yeah, they're good, but they're not a good as us, Sean - we're the best band in London.' That really got to me, I thought yeah, now that is a great attitude to have. But we were good though."

As the summer approached, and with Sean and Barry's insertion into the band only a month or so old, Tubeway Army and Beggars Banquet began to suffer from a very noticeable three-way musical division, which gradually became the hard-to-ignore elephant in the room.

"We had a split in the camp," recalled Gary, *"we had me and Paul on the one hand, who like me was very keen to get away from the punk thing, Beggars Banquet not being happy with what we were doing at all and Sean and Barry were firmly entrenched in playing punk for the rest of their lives. I could see, quite clearly, that the demand was for 'stars' again. The anti-star thing was over and it was dying."*

"Gary had started writing stuff like 'This Machine' when I joined but at the time we were getting punky types of bookings," Sean countered, *"Paul used to call it 'the weird stuff.' It didn't go down well at all. And that was the problem in the band. The weird stuff about machines just didn't go down very well with a punk crowd; they thought 'what the hell is going on?' It was like trying two totally different styles of music. I wanted to keep the audiences happy by playing the faster, heavier things such as 'Ice' and 'Do Your Best'.*

Martin Mills also sensed the growing rift among the members and began to voice his own concerns. *"The idea to bring Sean Burke in as rhythm guitarist never really worked. Not because Sean wasn't capable but his guitar style was exactly the same as Gary's. He played the same chords, not even different inversions of the same chords. So it just doubled up the sound. Although he was good in a way, it didn't really free Gary to do what he wanted to do."*

Those concerns had merit and would later be seen as prophetic, as the cracks within the band began to grow so large that they had become almost impossible to ignore.

"I stopped enjoying it," revealed Gary in 1987, *"it was like presenting it for a bloody exam, and they had to approve it."* 'They' being Sean and Barry.

Tellingly, Sean later mirrored similar thoughts, *"I felt frustrated in Tubeway Army. Gary was a bit of a control freak, I submitted ideas for the band, I wanted to write songs for the band but he wasn't keen on the idea. I wrote the opening riff to 'The Dream Police'. It was me that actually got that song started. The band drove it and Gary wrote the lyrics over the top. I was fed up that I didn't get any publishing on that, especially as the riff was my idea. At the time, however, I just didn't bother."*

With frictions quickly emerging on both sides, the end for Tubeway Army seemed inevitable and following a one-off show on 2nd June supporting The Ruts in Hayes, the unhappy foursome performed a trio of shows that would prove to be their last. The first took place at the Windsor Castle pub on the 17th, the second at the Hope & Anchor in Islington (where, as revealed in the Steve Malins book *Praying To The Aliens*, just three people showed up) then finally on 28th June, the band arrived at the White Hart pub in Acton.

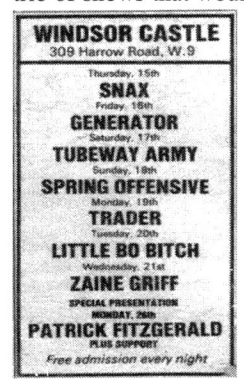

After the untimely demise of both the Roxy and the Vortex, the White Hart had begun hosting a weekly punk night called The Last Bastion Club, which quickly became a haven for the punk crowd. The pub however, was also a popular hangout for local skinheads, whose attitude and animosity towards outsiders was notorious. Prior to the show, Gary and the band had assumed that the The Skids were the evening's headliners. Unfortunately, when they arrived on the night for a sound check, both groups discovered a billing error. Tubeway Army had been listed as the evening's main event, which immediately ignited a heated exchange between the various members of the two groups. *"There was a mix-up on the bill,"* confirmed Gary when speaking to Peter Gilbert in 1986, *"it should have been the other way around. Somebody wrote the poster wrong!"*

The evening seems best remembered by local gig-goer Svenny Hoo Har, *"As a 16 year old punk rocker, I had to get out of the house in punk gear before my Dad got in from work - my Dad was an ex Royal Marine commando with a severe Victorian attitude to dress sense, so being a punk in 1977 was causing many family rows. Anyway I got to the White Hart early and witnessed the argument about who was top of the bill. Paul was adamant that they were the headliners as they now had two singles out and Jobson and*

Adamson were having none of it. Gary took a wide berth and protected his guitar, putting it behind the speakers. Then he left through a little side entrance door. There were about six of us and we went to listen to this argument between Paul and the Skids. Paul was assertive to the point of threatening and won the argument for going on as headliners. We had a laugh with him after that and helped him move amps and stuff and he gave me a Tubeway Army poster and he gave my friend a little bag of badges to hand out. He gave that to us for helping out and in his own words said something along the lines of 'it was you lot circling the Skids that made them give in.' I already had the Tubeway Army debut single and adored Bowie. I asked Paul 'where's your singer?' and he laughed and said he was probably out there hiding. I looked out of the entrance door and down the steps, onto the Uxbridge Road. Gary was speaking to some very posh woman who didn't want to go into the gig area because she thought it was incredibly rough and Gary just kept saying 'come on, come on' and laughing nervously."

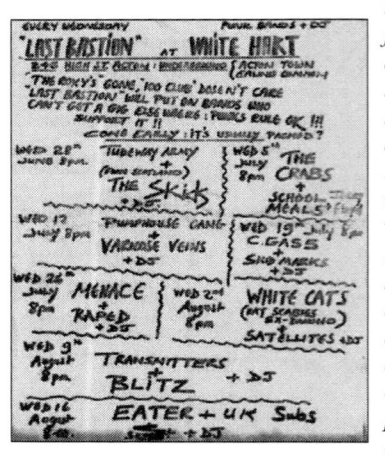

The Skids, who were far from happy about the headline error, begrudgingly went on first, performing their live set without incident. But when the time came for Tubeway Army to go on, the atmosphere had changed significantly; an ominously darker presence had arrived. Oblivious to this mood swing, a bleached blonde Gary counted the band in and the show began. But just four songs into their set, a fight suddenly broke out in the audience which temporarily halted the band mid song. Unsure of whether to stop for good or restart, Gary looked to Paul for guidance and they decided to continue with their set. But the fight didn't stop; in fact it turned extremely violent. Realising that the fight was about to erupt into something much worse, DJ Jerry Floyd took to the stage and stopped the band from playing, again pointing to the back of the hall.

Svenny revealed more of what he had witnessed to Stephen Roper via his website, The Touring Principle.

"The fight broke out while the band was playing, then the lights came on and the band stopped. The fighting continued and then suddenly stopped. Gary, I remember, turned to Paul and shrugged and they started playing again while the lights were still on. This only lasted for a minute

or so before the whole fight kicked off again and then that's when the band finally stopped for good. It was then obvious to all of us that there was a ruck going on at the back of the hall. The bouncers did nothing to help the two poor guys who were being beaten to a pulp by the Ealing skins."

With a full scale brawl taking place, the pub landlord had no option and reacted quickly by shutting off the power.

"The fight was stopped by I think, Jerry Floyd himself," continued Svenny, *"who physically grabbed the two guys and frog marched them out of the hall, giving them the chance to escape. Then there were stupid chants of Ealing, Ealing - but when we turned our attention back to the band they were already packing up, getting ready to leave the place."*

"The last gig Tubeway Army played was with The Skids at the White Hart in Acton," confirmed Sean when interviewed later about the night in question, *"I remember we had two PA systems on the stage because The Skids wanted their own PA system and of course we wanted our own. There was a fight in the crowd and I got hit in the mouth with the microphone when I tried to do a backing vocal. Gary freaked, he hated violence and would avoid it at any cost. I think we carried on playing and tried to ignore the punch-up hoping it might sort of stop but it didn't. Gary got slagged in the press afterwards about it. The weird thing is, at the end of the gig we went home in the normal fashion. I had no idea that Gary had decided he didn't want to do any more pub gigs."*

A week later on 8th July, a derogatory review of the show appeared in Sounds. It was written by Dot Garrhtt and read, *"Tubeway Army's singer has got Billy Idol's barnet, unfortunately he hasn't got his face, though he does best Peter Perrett hands down in the Lou Reed sing-alike stakes. The first couple of numbers were alright but it soon became apparent that all the songs were variations on a rather monotonous theme. The set was very short. Perhaps the intention was to return to rapturous applause and do a three song encore - it didn't happen.*

Halfway through the last number, a minor skirmish that had developed earlier erupted into something bigger. The house lights went on, the band continued playing. The management, who had obviously been on edge all night, signalled frantically to get the band to stop. Everyone's attention was directed to the back of the hall, then amid the confusion, the band started to play again. They were quickly shut up. It was by no means the worst fight I've seen at a gig, but just one guy getting his face pulped is enough to turn my stomach. OK - so its not the band's fault if there are a couple of morons in the audience whose idea of fun is punching someone's face in, but I have no respect for anyone who goes on playing as if nothing has happened. While you've got a microphone in front of you, you've got power; Strummer understands this and anyone who doesn't has got no place in a rock and roll band."

For Gary though, the fight was the final straw. He was no longer prepared to rough it on the pub rock circuit, churning out a blend of music for which he had absolutely no real interest. So the band's next scheduled show on 5th July at a local pub called The Brooke House in Hayes, Middlesex with label-mates The Doll, was immediately cancelled.

"There was an undercurrent of violence at a lot of the London pub shows at the time and realistically, the band wasn't expanding their audience playing these shows." reasoned Steve Webbon to me, during an interview, *"Also, I'm not sure Gary was too happy with the expanded line-up of Sean and Barry. Gary hated playing live and as a label we felt that was an important way to reach an audience. But he had a different audience in mind!"*

CHAPTER 11
AND I DISCONNECT FROM YOU

"Final bell in a disused music hall of laugher and mime"
(Lyric taken from 'Monday Troop')

By the middle of 1978, the punk movement was crumbling. The Sex Pistols had crashed and burned in July with their biggest hit single 'No One Is Innocent', a song 'sung' by the musically incompetent Ronnie Biggs, a notorious British criminal. (Biggs was on the run after escaping from prison for his part in The Great Train Robbery of 1963, but clearly couldn't hold a tune if his life depended on it). Live shows had descended into bloody scenes of violence as the National Front filtered through the crowds, distributing Nazi symbolism and racist propaganda. With high unemployment, inner city collapse, political stagnation and power cuts as well as food and oil shortages and frequent union strikes, there was still so much to be angry about in the UK. Unfortunately, this anger was being channelled in the wrong direction. Sensing that the punk movement was on its last legs, *Sounds* magazine ran a brilliantly written piece entitled 'New Musick', in which the writer pointed to a world beyond punk. The suggestion was that dub, electronic and disco would likely soon fill the gap, following punk's inevitable demise.

Although Gary's flirtation with synthesisers had only been brief, the electronica-pioneering German band, Kraftwerk, were onto their seventh studio album and in May, 1978, the band delivered what was widely regarded as their finest body of work thus far. Entitled *Man Machine,* the record saw the band evolving at a rapid pace, seamlessly marrying melody and technology across the album's 36 minutes. Kraftwerk's entry into the public consciousness had actually begun three years earlier with their surprise hit single 'Autobahn'. This song was so extraordinarily different to most of the contemporary music scene at that time and two groups paying close attention to Kraftwerk's stark synthetic endeavours were Sheffield's The Human League and Liverpool's Orchestral Manoeuvres In The Dark.

"When we heard 'Autobahn'", recalled OMD front man Andy McClusky, *"it was weird but it was very listenable. Their early music was quite experimental which suited us because we didn't have any instruments - a bass guitar which I got for my sixteenth birthday, an echo machine, a fuzz box, and things that Paul (Humphries) created which made noises but didn't actually have a keyboard attached. In the back room at Paul's mum's house, while she was at work, we made noises and fantasised about being the Wirral's answer to Kraftwerk. Punk was very*

useful to us. There was this attitude of just get up and do it. When punk came, we'd already found our alternative, I think we saw ourselves as synth punks."

While OMD were still very much finding their feet, The Human League, having formed a year earlier in 1977, were busy gearing up to record their first ever demo tape. That finished demo tape, featuring the future classic club anthem, 'Being Boiled', eventually came to the attention of former architecture student Bob Last, *"When I heard this phenomenal, fat bass riff in the middle of 'Being Boiled' it was like a mutant Bootsy Collins riff. I was like, 'God we've got to put this out' "*

Interviewed on the BBC show *I Love 1980*, The Human League's Phil Oakey revealed the reason why the band drifted so willingly towards an all encompassing electronic backdrop: *"I always thought that the synth thing was even simpler than punk; punk had to learn at least two chords or three chords, we didn't, we used tape recorders and we would use synths that you could set up like for a week in advance so when you finally pressed the button it sounded really impressive."*

'Being Boiled' eventually emerged as a single in June on Bob Last's Fast Product label with an interesting strap line, 'ELECTRONICALLY YOURS...' typed boldly across the single sleeve. Though not a hit, the song's underground impact was enough to prompt David Bowie to go on record, declaring that the band was *"the future of music"*.

However, with the exception of Kraftwerk and Ultravox!, it's unlikely that Gary would have been hugely aware of other synthesizer experimentalists like OMD and The Human League at this time, so low were these new bands' profiles. But like all of these new electronic artists, Gary had also seen a glimpse of the future and the race was now on to create something fresh, new and groundbreaking in pop music.

Three weeks after the band's last live outing, Beggars Banquet finally released 'Bombers' as a 7-inch single. Released on 21st July, reviews in the music press were generally negative and indifferent, with *Sounds* dismissing the song as *"sounding like a rough demo featuring a Billy Idol look-alike"*. Rival music rag, *Melody Maker* took a somewhat more diplomatic route, describing the A-side as *"Interesting if flawed. The song is hardly great but the treatment*

shows they're beginning to scour the studio for possibilities. The progression is well-paced and atmospheric, bolstered by some good old siren effects and undercut by some strident rhythm chops. A nifty blueprint."*

Frustratingly for the label, 'Bombers' failed to hit the mainstream singles chart and could only match the sales of 'That's Too Bad', again selling just 4,000 copies. The static sales figures were obviously deeply disappointing, especially as Beggars had made what was for them, a significant investment in the song's initial recording. But as discouraging as the sales were for the label, they were equally encouraging for Gary, as it reconfirmed to him that the punk movement in which he had been so deeply immersed, was quickly coming to an end. *"I was becoming increasingly convinced that I needed to move out of a punk band,"* Gary told Peter Gilbert in 1986, *"or that Tubeway Army as a band needed to move on. I didn't know at that point that the move would be into electronic music, I just knew I had to move somewhere. I became very frightened that the next big thing was going to come along soon and wipe away the remnants of punk. To me, punk was dying on its feet and I didn't want to be associated with it anymore. I wanted to be the next big thing. Paul was with me, the others wanted to stay punk."*

In the meantime, Sean, who was keen to get the band back on track after the White Hart debacle, visited the Webb family home shortly after 'Bombers' was released, to see what Gary and Paul were planning, now that there was a second single in the shops. *"I went around to his house a while later,"* recalled Sean, *"to see about a rehearsal and his Dad said 'that's it, it's over.' They told me that Beggars didn't want to pay the band a retainer. I was gutted. Then I found out that Paul had carried on working with Gary and they'd kept the name, Tubeway Army. I was very upset. I took it personally because Gary had sacked me basically and I felt I'd put a lot into Tubeway Army. I worked hard in Tubeway Army, me, Paul and Gary used to go out and have good times together."*

Gary saw things differently. Speaking to Peter Gilbert in 1979 for the fanzine *In The City*, Gary vividly recalled the final days of the line-up

53

that included Barry Benn and Sean Burke: *"We were playing gigs where no-one would turn up and Sean and Barry decided that they didn't want to do the new stuff that Paul and I were working on. Sean and Barry saw it as a sacking. It wasn't really. I just couldn't handle it the way it was. I didn't sack anyone; I'm not ruthless, just focused. I don't remember arguing with Sean or Barry about the split but I didn't want to force people to join me. It all seemed very clear to me, I was going somewhere else musically and they didn't want to go. So I went without them. Beggars' decision not to support Sean's new punk band was nothing to do with me."*

Sean vigorously disputes Gary's claim that he and Barry were 'entrenched in punk' claiming instead, *"I was just confused about where the band was going, plus I think I used to upstage him a bit and I got more birds than him which I'm sure pissed him off."*

Wherever the exact truth lies, there is at least one of Sean's claims that will forever remain a puzzle. Whether there is any truth to it or whether it was just a fit of pique, is still unknown, *"I once said to Gary about introducing a synth to the band but he would say 'Na, na, not for the band.' I had a Moog before I joined Tubeway Army and the first thing I learnt to play was 'Time Captive' by Arthur Brown's Kingdom."*

In August, the exiled duo quickly formed a new band called Station Boys with boxer Nick Combes inexplicably recruited on vocals. *"We recorded a track called 'No Time',"* Sean revealed, *"paid for by this management who then said we should call ourselves Tubeway Army. In the end they settled for Tubeway Patrol but it was obviously a cash in. I heard through WEA that Gary and Tony were very pissed off about it but it was nothing to do with me. We had this manager and he put us into Abbey Road Studios to do a single. The deal was that we had to be called Tubeway Patrol, I said no way, and I was totally against it. The rest of the band said that I*

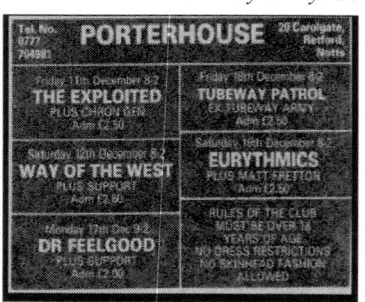

54

should think about it and of course they had a meeting and I was outvoted three to one. So, much to my disgust, we went along with it. I didn't believe in it because I thought we were good enough in our own right."

Gary later added, *"I thought that using that name was trying to rip off the fans. It seemed a little shallow and desperate."*

CHAPTER 12
TURNING POINT

"Look up, I hear the scream of sirens on the wall"
(Lyric taken from 'Bombers')

With Tubeway Army once again reverting back to just Gary and Paul, the duo entered a brief period of calm, allowing both musicians to further solidify their friendship. But for Gary, with a provisional album recording session only weeks away, he was still in a daze of uncertainty over the exact musical direction he wanted to pursue. This feeling was further exacerbated now that the punk element of the band had been confined to history. Although his embryonic work with synthesisers had succeeded in igniting a spark within him, the grand design of what lay ahead, was still not yet nascent. But that tiny spark was about to about to light an all-consuming flame.

Towards the end of the summer, a chance meeting with one of the band members of Ultravox! finally gave Gary the musical backdrop he'd been searching for. *"I first heard 'Slow Motion' by Ultravox! at a friend's party in the summer of 1978. Billie Currie was there although he wasn't well known then and I wasn't anything myself at that time. He brought along a copy of the record, I heard it and thought 'this is it', the synths integrated with guitars. They didn't replace them like Kraftwerk had done with just all electronics. That kind of thing didn't work for me."*

'Slow Motion' was without doubt the dawning of a new and exciting era in popular music and a real turning point for Ultravox! Listening to the track now, it's clear that legendary Kraftwerk producer Conny Plank had managed to significantly beef up the band's relatively thin sound. With 'Slow Motion' the lush wall of soaring synthesized sounds beautifully complemented John Foxx's moonlit bathed lyrics and otherworldly vocals. Plank had created a unique duel concept for the recording, a first in popular music, by merging stabbing synthesizer lines with pulsing guitars to create a thick synthetic haze, crowned by Foxx's distinctive and ethereal English voice.

With the musical fog in his mind finally lifted and a new direction beginning to come slowly into focus, Gary set about crafting a brand new and unique sound for Tubeway Army. *"I began to see an opening for a completely new kind of music, played in a completely new way. I'd been spending ages with my guitar trying to get it sounding bigger and more powerful so it was sort of, a bit, 'Eureka! There it is. That's what I've been looking for!' By this time, I was also thinking about going solo anyway and not being in a band anymore. The reason I started in a band* in the first place was because I lacked confidence to go out on my own. Now I was beginning to build up that confidence, having done two singles in the studio."

"I think we all knew that Gary was different," remembered Lurkers drummer Peter Haynes, "it was obvious that he was going to do something different; he just had something about him, charisma if you like. Although Gary stood out, he was very limited in what he was doing in a guitar-riffy band and I always used to say to him that he ought to revamp the old Bowie kind of thing, I never knew at the time that he had loads of ideas in his mind."

What was forming in Gary's mind was something that had never been tried in popular music before; pop music played not with the usual triumvirate of guitars, bass and drums, but instead with synthesizers as the main sound. *"The whole electronic thing had started taking shape in my mind. I was convinced that electronic music was going to shake the world."*

Re-energized and inspired after listening to Ultravox!'s enormously improved and hypnotic synthesized sound, Gary was now more anxious than ever to get back into the studio and begin crafting a sound that would in the space of a few short months, make him one of the most famous men on the planet.

CHAPTER 13
REBIRTH

"A drama is my perfect bride"
(Lyric taken from 'Basic J')

Sometime in late August, just prior to the band's scheduled visit to Spaceward Studios to record demos for the first official album, Gary's mother Beryl, arrived home with a surprise late birthday present for her son. *"My Mum bought me an old piano two weeks before I was due to go into the studio. I'd never even touched a piano before. She bought me an old second-hand upright which I started on at home. It was completely out of tune. I started to learn how a keyboard worked and how it went together. I also learned how to add bass notes to certain chords."*

Little by little, the pieces of the puzzle that had lain in Gary's mind for so long, slowly began to crystallize. With renewed enthusiasm to experiment further, Gary asked Martin Mills to hire him a Minimoog for the upcoming recording session, *"I started to work in August on a demo album. As all of my songs were guitar-based with chugging riffs I just converted it to the sound on this synth. I spent two days doing that. I started to get a little bit more confident about the way I was going and what I was going to be doing about it. I was looking very closely at the market where I was aiming, at the audience and what the audience wanted. I was just starting to think a lot more clearly and accurately about what was going on."*

Astonishingly, with Gary's prolific work-rate, the album sessions were completed in just two days. Gary also managed to steal some extra time to add more electronic elements to two of his newest songs, 'Listen To The Sirens' and 'Zero Bars'. The finished album featured a total of twelve tracks, (a thirteenth track, 'Fadeout 1930' which was a hurried rehash of an older song, 'Out Of Sight' had been set aside). Half of the songs earmarked for the album included vastly improved versions of previously recorded tracks that had been committed to tape earlier that year. Those songs included: 'My Shadow In Vain', 'The Life Machine', 'This Machine' (re-titled here as 'Steel And You'), 'Something's In The House', and 'Do Your Best' (re-titled here as 'Friends'). Gary later explained the reason for their inclusion. Speaking to journalist Paul Morley in 1979, Gary clarified why half of the *Tubeway Army* album consisted of songs he'd written during the ill-fated Mean Street era, *"I used some of the songs from that period on my first album. I was attracted to them like old photographs and I just wanted those songs out* to show them, if nothing else, there were a lot of revenge motives all over the place."

Science-fiction was beginning to feature even more heavily in Gary's lyrics at this point with the vastly improved reworking of 'The Life Machine' exemplifying Gary's futuristically creative imagination. *"I saw a programme once where there was this man looking down at his own body and he watched as the people came in to see him. Even though these people still love him, he's not quite the same. They love him because they are supposed to, and that is basically what this song is about. The torture is in the mind, where he can't go and yet he can't stay either. I was putting myself in the situation of the person who wants to die, he's in limbo and he can't go to heaven or wherever he's going, 'cos they won't switch the machine off that's keeping him alive. And he can't be in his body because he's dead. He's just sort of floating. I believe if somebody is dead, they should be turned off. I don't see any point in keeping somebody's heart going when they don't even know they're alive."*

Joining these revamped songs, were seven brand new compositions. As well as 'Listen To The Sirens' and 'Zero Bars', the album also included, 'My Love Is A Liquid', 'The Dream Police', 'Jo The Waiter', 'Everyday I Die' and 'Are You Real?' Of these, 'My Love Is A Liquid' was another track that benefited immensely from Gary's early synthesizer work. The song itself also strongly echoed Numan's fascination with the science-fiction genre.

"The song is about test tube babies, you fertilise them, put them in a tray and they grow. The line 'Did you know that friends come in boxes?' was actually about a future technology whereby a man could masturbate into a box of 'stuff' and from it, the child of his choosing would grow. A bit like add water and stir."

Two of the newer tracks, 'Are You Real?' and 'The Dream Police' dated from the latter days of the Sean Burke/Barry Benn era of Tubeway Army, with Gary describing 'Are You Real?' as *"a song about cloning, what might happen if you met your clone and the conversation that would go on."* As for 'The Dream Police', Sean later revealed an interesting twist to the songs lyrics, *"Gary wrote that line 'Junkies won't get radio time' on 'The Dream Police' because Beggars insisted we change one of the lyrics on 'Bombers' from 'junkies' to 'nurses'."*

'Everyday I Die' and 'Jo The Waiter' were both fairly stripped back acoustic songs, with Gary describing the latter as, *"Like 'Basic J', 'Jo The Waiter' was inspired by an ex girlfriend. Jo was actually a girlfriend, my first love or so I thought. It was a teenage thing, I was seventeen and it got very silly, but at least I got a song out of it. The storyline in the song is fictional although she did used to think I was a bit* strange apparently. I found that out long after she'd left. The reason for the gender uncertainty in the song was simply a clumsy attempt to cover up who I was singing about. At the time the only people that heard my songs were friends so I didn't want them to know it had anything to do with her."

The additional synthesizer parts found throughout the album came as quite a surprise to Jess Lidyard when he listened to the finished mixes. *"I left early because I'd done all my parts. When I heard it next, Gary had added keyboards to the songs. I was surprised but a lot of the material was still quite familiar."*

The album itself, further illustrated a band in musical transition, from nihilistic punk rock with the raw fury of 'Friends' to sadder and gentler acoustics like 'The Life Machine' and 'Every Day I Die'. But throughout the entire album, the musicianship remained faultless with Paul's hypnotically pulsing bass lines beautifully complimenting Jess's relentless drum skills.

A week after the recording sessions had been completed, the belated news of the band's split had finally filtered through the music press with *Sounds* and *NME* running brief news items regarding the band's demise. On 2nd September, the *NME* reported that *"Beggars Banquet still intends to release a group LP comprising demos, and lead singer guitarist Valeriun is now recording solo for the label."*

A similar piece printed in *Sounds* a week later on 9th September, reported that *"Tubeway Army, whose debut single 'Bombers' was released recently by Beggars Banquet, had split due to 'different musical directions'. Blond front man Valeriun remains under contract to pursue a solo career with an album planned for release later this year."*

When Beggars Banquet got the call from Gary, inviting Martin, Nick and Steve to come and listen to the final album mix, they were collectively taken aback with what they heard and actually, pretty unhappy with the result of the record company's investment. Gary explained, *"Because I had blond hair, the record company saw me as a pretty-boy, a punk-pop crossover act. When I came back with this weird electronic stuff they were furious. They'd originally signed me as a pop punk equivalent to The Lurkers and they wanted me to go in and do an album of punk songs; they were very upset when I didn't."*

Nick Austin seemed the most upset with Gary when he listened to the end result, *"Nick actually squared up to me in the office. I'm only little but I was so passionate I leapt out of my seat as well, we were going to have a fight. It was always a little bit strained with Nick. I used to get on best with Marty, maybe because Marty was more diplomatic."*

"I think that Nick still saw Gary as a 'punk' act," recalled Steve Webbon, *"and felt he should continue in that vein. Punk acts were*

expected to play live as it was the best way to build an audience. Nick wasn't 'against' Gary, it's just he was less willing to trust in his vision."

This tense period in Gary's life was also witnessed by Lurkers drummer Peter Haynes. *"Gary did have a few tense moments with Nick Austin over at Beggars Banquet but give the guy his due, he was definitely prepared to stand up for himself. When Gary went out to do the Tubeway Army album I don't think, initially, he got the support he needed. To be honest I don't think that Beggars Banquet understood what he was doing really."*

To further compound a now tense situation following the poorly received album playback, Gary delivered another unexpected shock to Martin, Nick and Steve. *"I told the record company I didn't want to be in a band anymore,"* Numan recalled, *"I wanted to be a solo artist. They didn't get it at all, they wanted a punk band and that's it. Luckily for me they didn't have any money because I'd blown the budget so they couldn't afford to send me back into the studio. Initially they said they wouldn't release it, so I said, 'Well, I'm not going back in, that's what I'm doing now.' Luckily they were a tiny little label and didn't have the budget to re-record it so they were just stuck with it. So they released it and it did a lot better than they expected."*

Steve Webbon, acting as unofficial peacemaker in the aftermath of the album playback, later expressed his own thoughts about the album Gary had delivered, *"Personally, I thought it was a good album and a progression from the earlier March recordings. I still like the rawness and directness of the recordings. However, the recent new recordings like 'Listen To The Sirens' and 'Zero Bars' showed that Gary was onto developing a different sound and was beginning to move on very fast."*

Press reviews, although scarce, were generally positive, with British music paper journalist Kelly Pike describing the record as, *"not the kind of album one surprises one's impressionable friends with for Christmas"* though she did admit to finding the record's *"infectious rhythms highly enjoyable."*

A more recent discovery in the following review clearly illustrates that there was much more anticipation about what was coming next from Gary, than was appreciated at the time.

RECORD BUSINESS DEC. - TUBEWAY ARMY : Tubeway Army (Beggars Banquet BEGA 4) Prod: Gary Numan Interesting exponents of the 'I am a machine' syndrome currently popular in what used to be called the new wave Tubeway Army proves to be an inventive threesome specialising in doomy words intoned over quirky, interesting riffs of the clockwork variety with occasional sorties into guitar or synthesizer solo territory which prove the band has the ability to take its ideas a step further. Gary Numan, lead vocals, guitars and keyboards also produced the LP and sounds quite a talent. Initial copies are in blue vinyl.

CHAPTER 14
THE WINDS OF CHANGE

"We could always go home but everyone says this is the place to be"

(Lyric taken from 'We Are So Fragile')

Following a four night run of shows at the Marquee, Ultravox!, the band with which Gary had become so enamoured during this period, released their third album on 8th September. *"Ultravox! were like the blueprint for what I was trying to do in my early years and John Foxx was my hero,"* Gary recalled in a number of online interviews, *"I thought he was a fantastic and enigmatic front man. I really loved what he did. The production on Systems Of Romance, compared to what I was doing, was just chalk and cheese. System Of Romance was probably the most important album to me in terms of how I wanted to approach electronic music, it was exactly where I wanted to go with my own music. They were the only people who were doing things where they mixed synthesizers and electronics with conventional instruments, and that's what I wanted to do. They were doing something that I'd never heard before; I wanted a conventional line up with a layer put on top it."*

Steve Webbon agreed, *"I think he had discovered the power that could be got from an analogue synth, then he looked at other contemporary bands that were using it. I think he liked John Foxx's image and the visual aspect as much as what they were actually doing with synths. I don't think he really discussed what he was trying to do, he was just very excited by the possibilities the synth created and demonstrated it with his own recordings."*

But as the dust began to settle from the record company's negative reaction to his album, Gary felt compelled to turn his attention towards yet another problem lurking ominously on the horizon.

"When I first began with the synthesiser after the guitar, I began to realise what a difficult instrument this was going to be if I was going to be a star with it. You can't run around the stage with it as you can with a guitar. It's not very interesting to look at, a great set of keyboards with this bloke behind it. So I decided that if it was to be the synthesiser for the main thrust of my music, I'd have to have a strong and different image to stand out."

In the weeks running up to the release of the debut Tubeway Army album, Gary and long time friend Nick Robson, began frequenting a new club that had just opened its doors in Soho, which played music that better reflected Gary's musical aspirations.

"We had become part of this wandering troupe of individuals," recalled Robson, *"who were going to clubs like Billy's, The Blitz, The Vortex, clubs that were started and frequented by people like Steve Strange, Boy George and Marilyn. There were also some very exotic women mixed in at these places, as well as all the flamboyant characters, so they were a big attraction to us too. Gary and I dressed fairly identically to go to the clubs at that time, mainly in a dark military style, many of our outfits like the Luftwaffe suits coming from 'army surplus' shops where we could buy a whole new identity for a couple of quid. But the music that was being played was outstanding; we were particularly entranced by the post-punk, clinical and experimental Germanic and Japanese sounds like Kraftwerk and Yellow Magic Orchestra and other bands who often had maybe just one great song like The Normal with 'Warm Leatherette'. This was mixed in with the usual suspects, Roxy Music, Japan and of course, Bowie, which made the music a veritable feast. But Ultravox! was also a huge favourite in this era and I think we first discovered their music at either Billy's or The Vortex and they became a staple of The Blitz. At this same time, Gary and I were going to a lot of small music venues like The Marquee, Dingwalls, Camden Palace and The Roundhouse. We'd see people like Siouxsie, Subway Sect and The Buzzcocks as well as the more refined acts like Ultravox! Looking back, it was an extraordinary era to be involved in but also an incredible treasure trove of new and very different material from truly unique and original artists."*

In January of 2013, when speaking to the website Phiadon.com, London-born artist Nicola Tyson described the opulent atmosphere that Billy's encapsulated. *"By 1978, a new scene was needed to fill the vacuum left after punk went mainstream and 'Bowie Night' was a start. Roxy Music and David Bowie had influenced the darkly flamboyant aspects of the London punk scene, and so in opposition to the dumb monochrome cynicism of mainstream punk, anything went each Tuesday at Billy's, the more theatrical the better."*

Though heavily seeped in nostalgia and theatre, Billy's, and later The Blitz, became gregarious and ostentateous homes for fashion, graphics, design, visual spectacle and of course exciting new music. In truth though, as a club, the interior of Billy's was every bit as grubby as both The Vortex and The Roxy, being essentially a subterranean dive located beneath a brothel. But despite its external lack of visual allure, the club quickly became a haven for music fans who had grown tired of punk's grungy guitars and repetitive anarchy. The idea to host what was to become known as *Bowie Night* was in fact the brainchild of the then unknown New Romantic pioneers, Steve Strange and Rusty Egan. *"One day,"* recalled Strange, *"Rusty and I were chatting about how things had gone a bit stagnant. We were talking about London clubs and comparing them to those in other cities. We were young and had the balls to do anything, so we looked for a venue where we could set up our own club. We were very shrewd. We went to Gossips, a club at 69 Dean Street, on a Tuesday and saw that it was empty. It was a venue with a great past - it had been known as The Gargoyle Club before the war. The people hanging out there were mostly Soho's sex workers, grabbing a breather. Two weeks later we went back to the owner and said we could pack the club. He could have the drinks profit and we would take the money on the door. Naively, it didn't occur to us for a moment that no-one would turn up. We printed up flyers with the tantalising line, 'Fame, Fame, Jump aboard the Night / Fame, Fame, Fame. What's Your Name?' We opened in the autumn of 1978 and very quickly we were successful. All the punks who were also closet David Bowie fans turned up."*

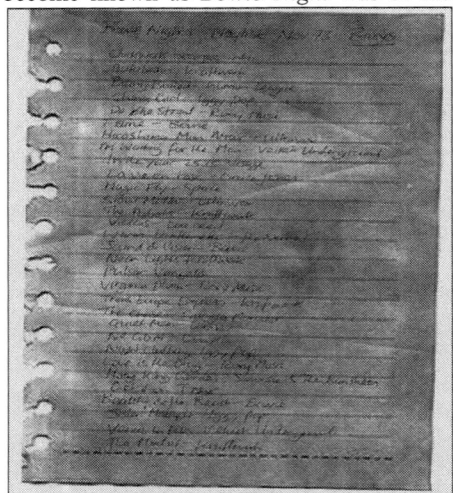

Soon enough, Billy's became a regular event and every Tuesday night, a flamboyant brigade descended upon the capital. The air inside was thick with an atmosphere of style and extravagant fashion, designed to shock and fascinate. Bowie Night proved to be the perfect antidote in the aftermath of punk with the music played being mostly German electronic pop from the likes of Neu! And Kraftwerk with pride of place taken by British artists Ultravox! and Bowie.

"Systems Of Romance," recalled Nick Robson, *"became the most played album in these clubs; 'Quiet Men', 'Slow Motion' and 'Hiroshima Mon Amour' were worshipped and revered as individual anthems. I will always remember when I first looked at who produced the album; I was amazed it was a female producer I'd never heard of before, Conny Plank. Female producers were rare then, rare even now but I just thought how cool this lady must be to be doing what she was doing with Ultavox! Of course, I didn't realize at the time that Conny was in fact a male German name."*

"Music had been stale for a long time," mused Gary in a later interview, *"punk had come along, turned the whole thing upside down and breathed a breath of fresh air into it but hadn't put anything of any class out. And that was the only thing that was missing: the one big star to come out of it that had seen it all going, learned all the lessons, and did something different that was musically competent, and somewhat different to what had been going on. The punk thing was dying quickly and nobody seemed to see what I saw, that as always, the public wanted a solo star that they could touch. The public was crying out for a solo singer, who behaved like a star. Punk was simply badly played heavy metal without the posing."*

In all, the Bowie nights at Billy's lasted three months before Strange and co were unceremoniously shown the door.

"They moved across to the Blitz in Covent Garden," remembered former Roxy and Vortex manager Susan Carrington, *"which was some kind of WW2 theme place, all propellers and that. But through Bowie and Kraftwerk they gave birth to the New Romantic movement."*

Nick Robson recently recalled that period, *"When Gary and I became members at The Blitz one night (I think we were maybe numbers 63 and 64), it was only on the approval of Steve Strange who guarded the club entrance like a hawk sitting poised on his throne and he was the style arbiter of who got in and who didn't. If he liked you and approved of how you were dressed and how you looked, you could become a member. If he didn't, you were out of luck and you had no chance of gaining entry. I guess he must have liked what he saw with Gary and I because we were immediately granted membership. But once we started going there each week and found ourselves bumping into members of some of the newly formed bands like Spandau Ballet and Culture Club, it was clear to see that we were witnessing the imminent birth of the New Romantics to a wider audience. At the same time, I could see that Gary, who at that time was still reasonably unknown, was standing on the precipice of a whole new movement and he was about to become a big part of it. This was an extremely exciting period and the feeling that a new era was dawning, was highly infectious."*

CHAPTER 15
WONDERFUL ELECTRIC

"You are in my vision, I can't turn my face"
(Lyric taken from 'You Are In My Vision')

As the release date for the *Tubeway Army* album approached, Gary's anxiety increased. That in itself was an added concern for Beggars Banquet who were already having a tough time reigning in their impatient signing; vetoing Gary's idea to call the album *Everyday I Die* as well as insisting that he keep the Tubeway Army name.

"For the first album, we at Beggars Banquet had a bit of a fight to get Gary to let us call it Tubeway Army," Steve Webbon remembers, *"because from Gary's point of view, Tubeway Army were gone. We thought it was a bit silly to throw away all the recognition that we had with Tubeway Army so we kept the name for the first album which was only really intended to be a demo tape anyway."*

"I was very keen to go off on my own now," Gary insisted, *"I didn't want to be part of a band, mainly because I was convinced that the public at large was sorely in need of a star. All the bands that were around, the magazines and the public were picking out the singers or the guitarists; they were picking out one person and focusing on them. There seemed to be little interest in featuring bands as a whole. But it seemed to me at the time that what people were after, and what people were missing, was a single singing star, a new one. Not an old one that was still going, but a new one, that would come out of the punk era, that would come from it with that kind of rebellion and something new but not quite so anti everything else. That's why I wanted to go solo. Not because I wanted to get away from Paul, or anything like that. No, quite the opposite. Paul agreed. Paul thought that's the way it should be as well. But Beggars Banquet didn't want to lose the small following that the band had, record sales-wise."*

With Beggars Banquet's decision to stay firm and hold on to the Tubeway Army name, Gary decided instead to change his own name.

"I thought that 'Valeriun' was extremely 'poncey', the name was obviously ridiculous, it was something I saw written on a wall as graffiti when I was driving to work in the mid 70s," explained Gary when talking to postpunk.com in 2014. *"So I scoured the Yellow Pages in the back of Beggars Banquet's offices and came up with 'Neumann', from Neumann Kitchen Appliances, I think. Took the 'E' off; took the 'N' off; and that's how "Numan" came about."*

The album, entitled *Tubeway Army*, with a sleeve designed by Steve Webbon, was eventually released on 15th November with a limited run of 5000 copies, all of which were pressed onto blue vinyl. Encouragingly for everyone, the record quickly sold out. Many people were to later to refer to the album as the Tubeway Army *Blue* album, although that was never an official title for it.

"It was a good reception for something like that," gushed the newly christened Numan in a later interview, *"there was obviously something there, an interest, which is why they then let me go ahead with the Replicas album. The first album was my first tentative steps, full of flaws, but first steps into electronic music. It was the keystone, the starting point for everything that was to follow. It was an enormously important record."*

With the album proving to be a success in unit sales, and reviews being generally positive, Gary turned his attention to his image.

"There were lots of people around playing synthesisers before me; Kraftwerk and Ultravox! were quite active when I came along in 1978. But they all looked so boring! Kraftwerk were never an influence although they were for a while, a name to attach yourself to which may be where this influence thing came from. I've never actually liked them very much."

In the meantime Ultravox! had managed to generate some much needed exposure for themselves when the band was given the opportunity to perform two tracks ('Hiroshima Mon Amour' and 'Slow Motion') on the influential music show, *The Old Grey Whistle Test* in late November. The performance was eventually screened on 5th December and following this, the band headed out on a UK tour playing London on 26th December. Cruelly though, Island Records suffered a sudden loss of faith in the band and dropped them just as they were about to tour the US, an important market where the band was just beginning to make an impact. Compounding this disaster, and unknown by any other members of the band, John Foxx, their enigmatic front man, had already been secretly making plans to leave.

"I'd decided to leave during the initial rehearsals for *Systems Of Romance*," recalled John Foxx, "*I urgently wanted to get on with a purer form of electronic music that became Metamatic. After all the touring, I'd realized I didn't want to be part of a band – even one I'd created. I had to wait out all the commitments for that album, then when the last gig was over I told everyone that was it. I gave them the Ultravox! name and caught a plane back to London and my wee store of synthesizers.*"

Foxx duly quit the band after a final show in the US at the Whisky A Go Go in March, 1979, sending the band into a lengthy period of uncertainty.

As the holidays beckoned, and buoyed by the fact that his synthetic endeavours were paying dividends, Gary was understandably anxious to get back into the studio to record the new songs he was feverishly writing. He was also more convinced than ever now, that any new material should be released under the name Gary Numan and not Tubeway Army, although Martin, Nick and Steve strongly disagreed.

"*They were very reluctant to put out another real album without the Tubeway Army name on it,*" recalled Numan, "*because they were scared to lose that small impetus which they had gained on that first album, which is quite understandable.*"

But despite the label's refusal to drop the Tubeway Army name, they did allow Gary, Paul and Gerald to return to the studio prior to the Christmas break. This time, Gooseberry Studios in Soho's Gerrard St. in central London was the chosen venue. Not wishing to waste this opportunity, the trio quickly laid down three of the brand new tracks Gary had written, 'Me! I Disconnect From You', 'Down In The Park'

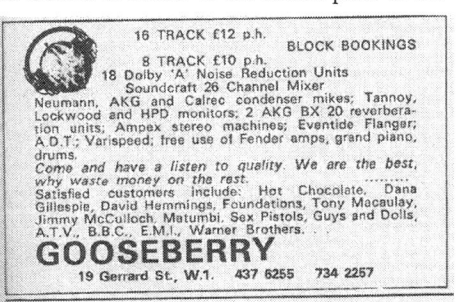

and 'The Machmen'. Delighted with the results, Martin Mills immediately booked the band back into Gooseberry to continued working on more songs with a view to the group recording a second album for the label, tentatively entitled, *Replicas*.

CHAPTER 16
REPLICAS RISING

"What will you make of my lines? What will you think I've said? What hidden secrets will you say are in my head?"

(Lyric taken from 'Critics')

For Gary, Paul and Gerald, 1979 had begun with a visit to the BBC's Radio 1 Maida Vale Studios in central London, where the band had been invited to tape a live session for the highly respected DJ, John Peel. Peel had previously aired selected tracks from the *Tubeway Army* album on his late night radio show in the run up to the Christmas break. Once there, the band duly cruised through three tracks, 'Me! I Disconnect From You' and 'Down In The Park' as well as an instrumental synthesiser piece entitled 'I Nearly Married A Human'. But while Gary, Paul and Gerald continued to hone the new songs Gary had written, a potentially catastrophic problem had unexpectedly reared its head for Beggars Banquet. *"We had changed our distribution deal to Island,"* Mills revealed, *"which was fine until they got into one of their perennial financial binds, so they did a license deal with EMI which meant that they were unable to help us any more so we were left high and dry until Warners did a license deal with us, giving us a cheque for £100,000 which was an unprecedented amount of money. Most of it went to pay unanticipated bills. Having a licence deal with Warners meant we sub contracted everything really, except the making of the music and the product managing of it, to a big global corporation.*

For Mills though, the cash injection couldn't have come soon enough. *"Every time we made a few quid in the record shops, Gary would want to spend it on a synthesiser. And his progress was only limited by the amount of money we could give him. All of this was happening at a time when we were financially pretty precarious. There was a point when we were bouncing salary cheques and were at the point of almost going bust. Warners saved us from bankruptcy to be honest, because we'd been running the record label out of the shops' cash flow and had pretty much reached the end of our ability to do that,"*

Having been given the go-ahead to record a second album, Gary set about persuading Beggars to buy him a synthesiser. *"Gary started bugging us to buy him a synthesiser,"* remembered Mills with a rye smile, *"we eventually bought him a Minimoog first, then a Polymoog, the first one cost £700 and the second one £1,500 and that was a huge amount of money for us in those days and we actually had to borrow the money to buy those machines. It was the purchase of those two synthesisers though that took him into another sphere."*

With recording of the album well underway, Gary spent some time fine-tuning his lyrics. He later explained to writer Peter Gilbert, the album's theme for the songs that would make up what would ultimately become *Replicas*. *"The reason for doing Replicas was that I wanted to start a new form of music which lyrically was interesting and would have some kind of class about it. Replicas was a definite concept, based on a character from the stories that I'd written prior to the album. I wasn't cut out to write a novel, I couldn't stretch it further than one chapter. The stories themselves were flawed but some of the basic ideas and imagery when converted into songs worked quite well. The whole concept of the album was basically that the government had decided they couldn't handle it anymore and gave the running of the country to machines. I used to read the newspapers about violence and about the way things were going in the world and it was just a very young man's view of what might happen in so many years time. The police force were no longer men, they were cloned machines; that's what the Machmen were. They were a super-elite police force, unbelievably strong and virtually indestructible. They had very white skin and were very strong. They were very powerful, arrogant and completely ruthless. The name "Machmen" came from an underground magazine called OZ that I was reading while I was at school. The album sleeve also depicted me as a Machman looking out the window at a 'friend'. I wore the make-up for the shoot because it was no good trying to be a Machman with a spotty face! I saw the city in Replicas bathed in constant light and everything was white. The walls of all the city buildings are light sensitive and glow as soon as it reaches dusk which meant there were no dark corners to hide in. In the stories, I visualised some of the metropolis in great detail. No humans, all machines, so it was clean, no dust, no pollution, nothing. In the society I was thinking about, there was a curfew and you weren't allowed out of your house or anywhere else after ten o'clock at night. Whatever entertainment you wanted for the evening, you would ring up for, you had to ring up for these peculiar half men/half machines to come along and they were called 'friends'. They were the same as Machmen, you couldn't tell if they were human or not. They always wore grey coats in my image of them, with grey hats and would always be smoking cigarettes to give off that nonchalant look. They did everything with ruthless efficiency and provided whatever you wanted, whether it was sex or playing chess. This man would visit your house in a grey coat and grey hat and the neighbours would never know the difference between him and a real human being. The machines eventually decided that the only thing that* was wrong with society, were the people themselves, so they thought they'd devise a way of getting rid of the people without the people realizing it. So they invented a thing called a Quota Test. The men were called 'Grey Men'. They would come around and basically give you an I.Q. test. If you didn't come up to scratch, you were taken away and supposedly re-educated from the machine. What you were in fact, was just gotten rid of. What people didn't realize was that every month when a Quota Test would come around it was more difficult than the one before. So, bit by bit they'd get rid of all the people like an hour hand on a clock, so slow that people wouldn't notice until it was too late. Anyway, that was the theory behind that. There were people called 'Crazies' who lived under the city and had suspected what was going on and ran. I got the image for Replicas one night I was out; I went out to a club once and there was a bloke walking around all dressed in black and I thought 'Christ, that looks good' so I got the image from him really, I got some of the titles for the album from a William Burroughs novel so basically I just put all these pieces together."

"Replicas was one of those albums that you just knew was going to be a hugely important piece of work," recalled Nick Robson,

"I remember watching Gary use a Minimoog at the studio in Soho where he was recording the album, and just being gob-smacked by the sound that came out. The same experience was later felt when I first heard him use a Polymoog and then later the Arp Odyssey. But after all these years, Replicas still sits in my top five favourite albums, it just never gets old."

"I had the most fun making Replicas because I wasn't successful - I had nothing to lose and everything to gain," recalled Numan fondly in a later interview, "it was incredibly exciting as I'd been signed and the whole world was on offer really. Everything about being in a studio was

new; I was learning a huge amount every second I was in it. Everything seemed fresh and it was the most amazing period to make records in."

With the band's second studio album having been completed in just 5 days, (and rumoured to have cost little more than £500) Martin Mills decided to check on the label's investment. He gathered a select group of Beggars employees and attended one of the final mixing sessions that was taking place at Marcus Music, a tiny 16-track studio in Portobello Road in London's Chinatown district. Though Mills was familiar with the tracks that had been recorded so far, he was stunned when the master tapes rolled and he heard 'Are 'Friends' Electric?' for the very first time. *"I remember going in very late during the mixing sessions and although we'd heard all the other songs before, we hadn't heard 'Are 'Friends' Electric?' until it was already recorded. They played it to me and I thought immediately that it was just an amazing and mesmerising song."*

"The song was basically about how life in the near future would be," enthused Gary in a later interview, *"a world of personal alienation. The song was inspired by living in tower blocks in England; I was feeling very de-personalised at the time. It was written on an old piano. It's actually two different songs put together. I had a verse for one and a chorus for the other but I couldn't finish either, but I realized they sounded all right stuck together. That's why it's five minutes long. Before I recorded It, I was playing it back and I hit the wrong note and it sounded much better. That harsh note is probably the crucial note in the hook. It transformed it from almost a ballad into something quite unusual. The spoken part was about an incident that happened at Christmas 1978. It speaks for itself, S.U. was a person. The rest of it is about the theme, where you can buy friends - you hire them by the hour. They're electric. You ring up and say you want a friend for something - it can be for sex, for talking, whatever you want and they'll send one along. The girl in the song (Sue Wathan) gave me a book called The Magus which has left me paranoid to this day and the paranoia started with her. It was only intended as a simple gift but I'm sure that it was all part of a plan to mess with me. I'd always been fairly distrustful of people before and that book just about finished me off. I wasn't completely electronic at this point either. 'Are 'Friends' Electric?' for instance had distorted guitar all over it."*

The line in the song's first verse, *'There's a man outside, in a long coat, grey hat, smoking a cigarette'* also had a particularly poignant significance for Gary. *"That was all inspired by a ghost I saw with a mate of mine on the Piccadilly line. I was on my way to buy my first proper guitar and coming out of the station there was a bloke about three steps up from us on the escalator. As we got to the top we followed him around to the left and it was blocked off. There was a wall and he had disappeared."*

> TELEX FROM BEGGARS BANQUET TO WEA RECORDS (MARCH 1979) ON COMPLETION OF REPLICAS RELEASED 4TH APRIL 1979, ARE FRIENDS ELECTRIC RELEASED 5th MAY 1979.
>
> 261425 WEAREC G
> ATTN DAVE JARRETT
> MARCH 28
> RE. TUBEWAY ARMY
>
> TUBEWAY ARMY? IT PRESENTS A CONFUSING PARADOX, BECAUSE TUBEWAY ARMY DISBANDED IN JULY 1978 YET HERE IS THE NEW TUBEWAY ARMY ALBUM. BUT DIDN'T THE FIRST ALBUM OPEN WITH AN EPITHAPH TO TUBEWAY ARMY ON 'LISTEN TO THE SIRENS'? AND AREN'T THE MUSICIANS THE A SAME AS ON THE VERY FIRST SINGLE? WELL YES, BUT TUBEWAY ARMY IS REALLY GARY NUMAN WHO CURRENTLY WRITES, PRODUCES, SINGS AND PLAYS ALL THE INSTRUMENTS EXCEPT BASS (PAUL GARDINER) AND DRUMS (GARY'S UNCLE - JESS LIDYARD). WHEN THE GROUP STOPPED LIVE APPEARANCES AND 2 MEMBERS LEFT, THE TUBEWAY ARMY NUCLEUS SPENT THREE DAYS RECORDING DEMOS WHICH HAD SUCH BRILLIANT UNPOLISHED ACCESSIBILITY THAT BEGGARS BANQUET RELEASED THEM AS THE FIRST ALBUM IN A 5,000 LIMITED EDITION WITH NO BACK UP PUBLICITY OR MAJOR DISTRIBUTION. REVIEWERS EITHER IGNORED OR WERE FAVOURABLY CONFUSED BY THE STRANGELEY ATTRACTIVE AND COMPELLING MUSIC BUT, WITH THE SUPPORT OF SPECIALIST RECORD SHOPS AND FANZINES (HERE AND ABROAD) AND A GRADUAL GROWING AWARENESS OF THE MUSIC, A CULT FOLLOWING HAS BUILT UP AROUND TUBEWAY ARMY AND GARY NUMAN.
>
> THE NEW ALBUM 'REPLICAS' USING THE SAME MUSICIANS, PRESENTS THE PROOF THAT GARY NUMAN IS ONE OF THE MOST POWERFUL NEW TALENTS TO MATURE OVER THE LAST 18 MONTHS. MORE MELODIC AND STRUCTURED THAN THE LAST LP, THE MUSIC RETAINS ITS CHILLING STARKNESS BUT HAS A NEW DEPTH AND STRENGTH IN ITS DECEPTIVE SIMPLICITY AND ACCESSIBILITY.
>
> GARY IS CURRENTLY WORKING WITH AN EXPANDED GROUP ON A THIRD ALBUM ('THE PLEASURE PRINICPAL') AND PREPARING TO PLAY LIVE AGAIN, THIS TIME NOT AS TUBEWAY ARMY BUT AS HIMSELF - GARY NUMAN........ SO ENDING THE PARADOX OF TUBEWAY ARMY.
>
> DISCOGRAPHY
> AS TUBEWAY ARMY
> SINGLES: THAT'S TOO BAD / OH DIDN'T I SAY (DELETED)
>   BOMBERS / O.D. RECEIVER / BLUE EYES (DELETED)
>   DOWN IN THE PARK / DO YOU NEED THE SERVICE? BEG17
>
> ALBUMS: TUBEWAY ARMY BEGA 4 (UNAVAILABLE)
>   REPLICAS BEGA 7
>
> BEG 17T A 10 INCH VERSION ALSO FEATURING A GARY NUMAN SOLO TRACK 'I NEARLY MARRIED A HUMAN'

CHAPTER 17
THE CALM BEFORE THE STORM

"The question now is time, the hours pass so slowly, I know we're moving out of line, but that's the risk you're taking with me"
(Lyric taken from 'Check It')

With *Replicas* mixed and mastered by the early spring, the first fruits from the album arrived on 16th March when Beggars released Numan's favourite song, 'Down In The Park' as a single. Described by Mills as 'chillingly dramatic' the lyrical inspiration behind the track actually had its origins in a 70s comic strip Gary had read at Ashford Grammar School. It depicted terrifying creatures that were half human, half machine, and oddly, a similar idea that later formed the backbone of the hugely successful Terminator movie franchise. *"They were incredibly powerful machines,"* remembered Numan when speaking to Ray Coleman in 1982, *"with skin that was human, tailor-made and designed and genetically engineered to fit and be put onto the machine. The only way you could tell they were different from humans was their eyes, they had a horizontal bar instead of a circular pupil and they could see with great clarity for many miles."*

When reviewed in the pop weeklies, journalist Joe Philips was full of nothing but praise, gushing, *"Check out the atmospheric single 'Down In The Park' and experience this technologically emotional music."* Fellow scribe Gunga Din, writing for a rival magazine, voiced similar sentiments when reviewing the single: *"Gary Numan's Tubeway Army may be besotted with the eerie subterranean wastelands of Burgess and Bowie but they can keep a spectre alive. If it doesn't make you look over your shoulder in horrified disbelief, then you're a better man than I."*

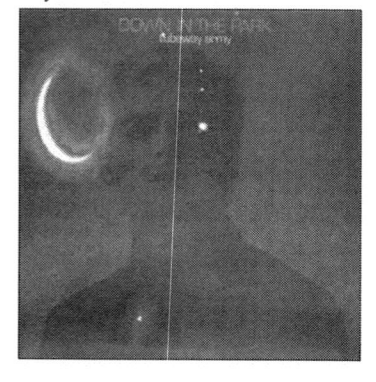

For the album though, the song was lyrically tailored to follow the story set out in *Replicas*. As Gary explained, *"'Down In The Park' was about the machines in the park; these machines turned on with light sensors. They turned on when the park grew dark and there was no light, and they were allowed to do anything they like. They were all programmed for horrific crimes against people. See, if people were out at that time of night, the machines would destroy them in all sorts of obscene ways. That was a deterrent to stop people coming out. And also if you were caught by them, you shouldn't have been there anyway, so you had no comeback against them. So in theory, there was nothing wrong with the machines because you shouldn't have been out there in the first place."*

Although the single didn't make any real impact on the UK singles chart, it was becoming clear that Numan's icy, synthesised approach was quickly gaining interest and more crucially, a following, particularly at London's hippest club The Blitz. *"It didn't get any radio play,"* Numan remembered, *"but it sold ten thousand copies. It seemed like an enormous figure to me, and I think Beggars were very pleased about it and were very encouraged by it. Especially since they had got an album done in less than five days which was recorded very cheaply; it must have meant that they got their money back on that one single alone. And all of a sudden, something's happening here. This electronic thing is taking off. The single was quite well received. It's probably the only single that I ever got good reviews for in my life! And then the album came out which initially didn't do much: just a few thousand copies."*

Press reviews for *Replicas,* though scarce, did reveal the first signs that the emergence of electro pop was in for a bumpy ride with journalist David Hepworth moaning that *Replicas* was *"a long way from the concentrated pop of Bowie and even Ultravox!"*

Pop writer Chris Westwood took a different view finding much to admire in the record, musing: *"Gary Numan has restored my faith in the future, he plays modern music which does not leave me cold, every song is a real melody with controlled keyboards and android vocals, Simplistic synthetic beat music, relying heavily on structure and melody. Tubeway Army's*

approach puts them, inevitably, in a clique. But they are sufficiently adept and individual to secure their own corner within it. How seriously Numan takes all this humanoid robotic mouthwash remains to be seen but then who am I to complain? I like his record. When the machines rock, they will sound like this."

At the same time *Replicas* was available in record shops, Tubeway Army's self-titled debut album from the previous year had caught the attention of music producer, Ronnie Bond, a man who was at the time heavily involved in the making a new television commercial for Lee Cooper Jeans. With the jeans company demanding a new wave style track to accompany their latest jeans campaign, Ronnie approached Beggars with a view to utilising Gary's voice for the upcoming commercial.

"Ronnie heard my voice as my publisher was playing the first album one day. He had the next office so he asked who I was and got in touch with me that way. When I was asked to do it, it had already been done. I just went along to the sessions. I didn't write the music or the lyrics, I just sang it. I got forty quid for that, a lot at the time for me. I was getting eighteen quid a week and to get forty quid for half an hour's work was amazing. I remembered I said to the man then, 'Would it ever be a single?' because at that point I wasn't famous. And he was very offhand about it and just put me down a little and said, 'Yeah, we might, we might not. We'll let you know.' That sort of thing. It made me feel a little bit small. I never signed anything, I just went on and did it, got my money in my hand and out I went. So yeah, I was well turned over because apparently what you should get is like a royalty on iteration. A session rate for doing that was much higher than forty quid anyway at that time. But I didn't know - to me forty pounds for a session seemed like an awful lot of money."

CHAPTER 18
ARE 'FRIENDS' ELECTRIC?

'Everyone heard the voice on the radio.'
(Lyric from 'The Machman')

"Hypnotic and highly recommended, surely a hit?"
(Magazine review for 'Are 'Friends' Electric?')

"One of the most exciting new bands I've seen in a long time."
(DJ Kid Jensen introducing Tubeway Army on Top Of The Pops)

"I had a No. 1 single with a song about a robot prostitute and no one knew. I've kept the piano that I wrote it on, it doesn't work anymore but I'll keep it forever."
(Gary Numan)

"He saved our bacon. If it were not for Gary Numan I wouldn't be sitting here."
(Martin Mills)

With Warner Brothers now handling the Beggars Banquet record distribution, Martin Mills felt confident enough to issue a second single from the album, choosing the one track that he'd found all along to be the most enthralling, *"'Are 'Friends' Electric?' was really long and a ludicrous choice as a single in every conventional sense but we all along regarded it as a vehicle to sell the album and released it as a single anyway, it was such an irresistibly good song."*

But although Gary was pleased to see Beggars changing tack and getting behind him to support the new album, the second single choice initially baffled him, *"I couldn't see any way that the song could be a hit. It just didn't seem like a chart single, it was too different, too much away from straight pop. My ambition at this point was to try and sell out The Marquee."*

With 'Are 'Friends' Electric?' scheduled for release in early May, Beggars sent Gary away to shoot the cover for the single's picture sleeve. *"When I was commissioned to do Gary's make-up for the sleeve of 'Are 'Friends' Electric?'* recalled make-up artist Mary Vango in 2014, *"I started off by listening to the music. Gary had caught the zeitgeist, the new mood for electronic sounds, but was doing his own thing with it. I worked with a lot of musicians in the 1970s and 80s, but Gary always stood out: he seemed the most unreachable. Where David Bowie was theatrical, Gary was more otherworldly – remote, but not aloof or arrogant. He was terribly shy and couldn't make eye contact. We spent an entire day in the dressing room, and I don't remember a single bit of conversation. I imagined him as someone who never saw the sun – not because of lots of partying, but because he seemed so disconnected from nature. I wanted his skin to look pallid, so I used a very light base. To make him look weary, I put on lots of dark, heavy kohl. He had to seem like a very complicated character: dark and remote, but not sinister, just cut off from his emotions. At the back of my mind was a Stanley Kubrick film I'd been really taken with, Barry Lyndon, which was set in the 18th century and shot in candlelight. I'd been wanting to use that look on someone for ages – then Gary came along."*

'Are 'Friends' Electric?' was released on 4th May with the first 20,000 copies being made available in a unique style of merchandizing. *"Warner Brothers had just introduced this new technology, the 7-inch picture disc,"* recalled Mills, *"they'd only made one picture disc before so the second one was 'Are 'Friends' Electric?' which meant it was going to be released initially in this hugely desirable and collectable format."*

Whether the picture disc format was a perfectly timed stroke of luck or just masterful planning, all 20,000 picture discs were quickly sold out in the space of just two weeks, propelling 'Are 'Friends' Electric?' into the lower reaches of the UK singles chart. With this latest positive response to Gary's new style of music, it became clear that the band would need to go out on tour to promote the single and the album. This would be Numan's first live shows since the White Hart fiasco of 1978. At the same time the single entered the charts, Gary, Paul and Gerald had begun to audition some new band members as Gerald had made it clear to both Gary and Paul that he didn't want a full time career in music.

"I started the auditions for the keyboard players in the basement of the Fulham Beggars shop before 'Are 'Friends' Electric?' was a hit. Gerald was there with me as he was the one picking the best drummer. I'd just play 'Are 'Friends' Electric?' or 'Down In The Park' and they'd just play along to it. Simple as that really. Cedric Sharpley turned up at the auditions and was obviously a brilliant drummer from the moment he started. Gerald was very impressed, so Cedric got the job. I also needed two keyboard players because I didn't intend to play keyboards at that time on stage and two people showed up, Chris Payne and this French man."

"I had finished music college and I was working as a temp for our local council taking down trees," remembered Chris, "and I turned up in a donkey jacket and work boots. When I saw this 'new wave' looking band I thought, 'Shit!!! I don't have a hope in hell of getting this gig!' I had *never played a synth before. Bluffed my way through the audition pushing every note under the sun and making it look as if I had a clue. The real bonus for me was playing the viola and Gary, being a big fan of stringed instruments, loved the sound. Luckily for me, Gary saw my potential as opposed to my dress sense."*

"Chris conned me," laughed Numan, still amused by the memory, *"he turned up and said he knew all about keyboard synthesizers. And apparently he'd never seen one before in his life, which I finally found out later. He turned up in Wellington boots, a moustache, and his college scarf, a tremendous character. And there was another bloke who turned up too, a Frenchman. Chris could play well, actually he absolutely fooled me that he knew all about synthesizers. The Frenchman I really couldn't understand at all, and apparently on the day, he had diarrhoea or something and every five minutes he kept disappearing off to the toilet and being sick from both ends! He had the habit of bending over and playing the keyboard with his eyes about three inches away from his fingers. 'Down In The Park' is five notes, you know, the main verse. It's the simplest thing in the world to play, and he couldn't get it right so that was the end of him. After that, we had to go out and find another keyboard player. At that time because Ultravox! had just split up I came across Billie Currie and he eventually became the second keyboard player.*

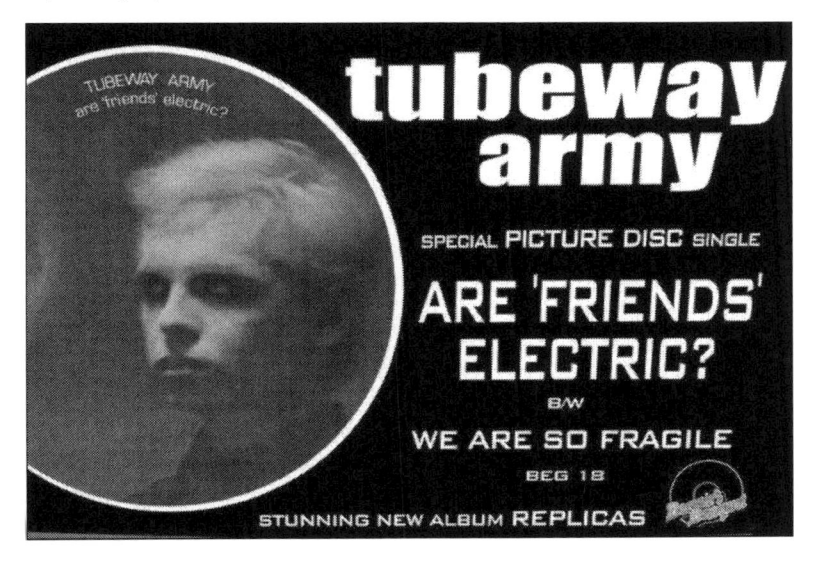

With the novelty of the picture disc proving to be a big seller, the newly constructed band suddenly found that Tubeway Army was very quickly becoming the next big thing. *"I remember Gary driving me back home once"* recalled Billie Currie, *"and he said 'This is the new single' and he showed me the picture disc for 'Are 'Friends' Electric?' And it was good; I suppose I was quite jealous really. The next minute it was an absolutely massive thing, it was absolutely huge."*

With the single landing just outside the all important top 40 at number 48 in its third week of release, the acclaimed late night, live music show, *The Old Grey Whistle Test*, made contact with Beggars Banquet, inviting the band to perform two tracks on the show. The speed at which Tubeway Army was now moving was something not lost on one of its new members.

"After the audition I remember events moving very swiftly," revealed keyboardist Chris Payne, *"and before I knew it, we were in Shepperton rehearsing for The Old Grey Whistle Test, a live BBC TV music show that used to broadcast every Tuesday night."*

Gary further revealed, *"The picture disc had got to No. 48 in the charts by this time and we got to do The Old Grey Whistle Test. Our appearance was a part of their new policy and we were the token new wave band that week. It was still Tubeway Army at that point, but I was Gary Numan within Tubeway Army."*

For their imminent TV appearance, Gary opted to expand on the visual theme he'd created for the *Replicas* album. He dressed the entire band in uniform black, as visually, he was determined not to repeat the mistakes that previous electronic/synthesiser acts had made when appearing on TV, by looking either drab and boring or just plain weird. The idea behind the somewhat sinister all-black look was something Numan had chanced upon when glancing through a collection of old WWII magazines. *"The whole image was from the Nazis,"* he told Ray Coleman in 1982, *"my idea was of a super police force which looked the part in jet black."*

With the visual styling settled, Gary later expressed his satisfaction that although he felt he'd done all he could to give 'Are 'Friends' Electric?' its best shot of an entry into the UK pop charts, dreams of superstardom were just about the furthest thoughts from his mind.

"I just saw it as making myself known at quite a low level for doing something unusual and classy. And that was all I saw it as doing. I considered what I was doing to be quite innovative, to be quite new. I wasn't that modest about it, but I certainly didn't think it was particularly worthy of great fame at that point. As I say, I saw the next pop star coming as being more commercially orientated, more chart orientated."

Gary's invitation to *The Old Grey Whistle Test* wasn't without its sacrifices though, because it meant having to cancel his imminent holiday plans, as Nick Robson explained. *"Gary, my brother Garry and I had just booked a vacation to go to Greece and Gary phoned one day, a week before we were due to travel and said, 'I can't go, we're doing The Old Grey Whistle Test'. Now you have to understand that The Old Grey Whistle Test at that time was like The Holy Grail of the British music industry, it was legendary, every boy's dream. It was such an honour to be asked to play on the show, there was no way you'd ever turn it down, not for anything. But it was weird, we were just about to go on a cheap package holiday to get brown and find girls and suddenly Gary had this offer of a lifetime. So my brother and I went on the trip because we couldn't afford to cancel. We came back home with Mediterranean tans and in the interim, Gary had turned ultra white and had become a star."*

On the day they were due to perform, an understandably nervous Gary joined the rest of the band on one of the show's soundstages and waited for their allotted spot. *"I remember being very frightened."* Numan later revealed, *"I remember rehearsing for days and days and days. Every single movement in the early days I used to practice, a movement for every line, and I'd rehearse it. I wasn't the slightest bit natural at all. So when people said that I was very wooden on stage, at the time I was very upset about it. I thought it was unfair, but they were quite right, I was, very wooden, very inexperienced on stage. And I probably looked every bit as ill at ease as they said I did. If I didn't plan how I was going to move I wouldn't move. See, I'd never been on stage without a guitar; always had a guitar, so you had somewhere to put your arms, for a start. You didn't have to move because you only had a guitar and you had to stay with the microphone because you were singing. Now all of a sudden I'm on live television, I've got no guitar, I've got to do something with my arms, you know?"*

"It was our first show together as a new group," explained Chris Payne in a later interview,*" and we were obviously very apprehensive. It didn't help matters that the other guests, The Scorpions, played just before us, and at the end of their set a crane camera moved back to get a wide shot and took down one side of our PA system. Imagine the panic as it was live! It did end well though."*

Sitting at home in Liverpool watching the taped performance on TV was Andy McClusky, whose own synth-based duo Orchestral Manoeuvres in the Dark were also making their first steps towards mainstream recognition.

"I remember seeing Gary on The Old Grey Whistle Test and going 'F**k! There's another person from England doing it.' We'd never heard of him at that stage. 'Who's this Johnny-come-lately bloke from London?'

There was probably also a little bit of frustration and jealousy from all the other synthy bands, like The Human League and Ultravox! who'd actually been going longer than Gary had."

But for Gary, the reality of appearing on a show he'd watched for years, was more than a dream come true: *"Just being on it, to me, was something I'd always dreamed of. I couldn't believe it. I mean, one week I wasn't doing anything, the next week I was on The Old Grey Whistle Test."*

But no sooner had the cameras stopped rolling, when news came through that the band had landed themselves a second piece of good fortune, as Chris Payne explained: *"Later that evening we were told that a spot had come up for us on Top Of The Pops, which at the time was the 'God' show for music as MTV etc didn't even exist then. It was a frantic few days and as it was happening, I think we all sensed that something was about to happen."*

Top Of The Pops was usually recorded on a Wednesday and broadcast the following day. The band's inclusion on the show (listed as Thursday, May 24th) was courtesy of a new feature that, for the first time, took a look beyond the UK top 40 singles chart to showcase a new act hovering just outside the main chart.

"At that time, Top Of The Pops was doing a thing called 'Breakers', remembered Gary, *"where they would play one song from outside of the chart that was showing significant movement. What happened was that Simple Minds also had a similar kind of thing going on; they were just on a big tour with the band, Magazine. So, they had to pick one of us. They were more unknown than I was so they picked me. So, the picture disc was enormously helpful in getting us to that point. I mean, I wouldn't have been there without it."*

For the band to perform on both *Top of the Pops* (apparently at the suggestion of DJ John Peel) and *The Old Grey Whistle Test* in the same week was unheard of at the time especially for a relatively unknown band. But it was the kind of exposure most artists dream about. Billy Currie agreed, *"It was amazing luck for Tubeway Army to have the single played twice on television in the same week because it just escalated from there."*

"I certainly think the way we presented ourselves on Top Of the Pops was enormously important," Numan recalled when asked in a later interview about his first national TV appearance, *"because when I went there, I said, 'I don't want any of your coloured lights, I want all white lights because I'm going to be all in black and I want a lot of white light coming up from the floor.' I was very intimidated by the actual performance which is one of the main reasons I didn't smile. It wasn't part of the image, I was just very frightened and very nervous. We had*

one of Chris's friends on guitar who did that one show for The Old Grey Whistle Test, and I think he did Top Of the Pops the following day because he did them one day after the other and I never saw him again. I don't know what happened to him."

There is no doubt that the group's startling appearance on the show, hosted by DJ Kid Jensen, created an immediate and enormous swell of interest particularly towards Gary as an individual persona.

"The first time he was on Top Of The Pops, I think either I phoned her (Joanne) or she phoned me," remembers Susan Sully of The Human League, *"and I said 'have you seen this man on the telly - he's fantastic!'"*

Following the band's *Top Of The Pops* debut, 'Are 'Friends' Electric?' jumped from the No. 48 position in the charts all the way to No. 25. The following week (7th June) the single climbed a further five places to No. 20 (prompting a second *Top Of The Pops* appearance), then a week later to No. 7, where the band again performed on *Top Of The Pops*, and then incredibly to No. 2.

"When it got to Number 2," explained Gary, *"it was such a dream come true that I wouldn't let myself believe it'd get to Number One so that I wouldn't be disappointed if it didn't."*

On the week beginning 25th June, 1979, when the official charts were unveiled for the first time, 'Are 'Friends' Electric?' had done what neither Gary nor his record label could have ever imagined, climbing that one final place to the coveted No.1 slot.

"I was sitting at home watching television and I got a phone call from Martin," revealed Gary in a later interview, *"he just said, 'You've done it.' I said, 'What?' He said, 'You've got to Number One.' I said, 'Oh, good.' And that was that."*

"Gary's whole profile just caught the public's imagination," Mills explained, *"after we got him on Top Of The Pops and The Old Grey Whistle Test in the same week, which you weren't meant to do because one was for albums and one was for singles, 'Are 'Friends' Electric?' flew up to the top of the chart. It was amazing, just fantastic! I was at Warners' Broadwick Street offices on the Tuesday morning when the news came through. I remember it knocked Anita Ward's 'Ring My Bell' off the number one slot, it was really exciting. None of us could believe it that 'Are 'Friends' Electric?' should reach No.1; it astonished us as it was such an off-the-wall song to do it. Five and a half minutes long, it's got no obvious tune and no-one knows what it's about, but it's an absolutely fabulous piece of music. It literally changed our lives."*

(Top of the Pops sound check, Tubeway Army's debut appearance.)

Gary added, *"When it did happen, I was still in the same house. I didn't have a whole lot of mates although I had a girlfriend at the time. My family have always ended up being my best friends, really. And that was lovely, to celebrate with them. You sort of imagine there will be showers of gold dust and money and Page Three girls lining up at the door and an instant assortment of flashy cars in the front garden that miraculously appear. It was though, very much an anti-climax."*

"My reaction to it going to Number One was one of total disbelief," remembered Steve Webbon, *"I remember we got a telegram from WEA that said 'Welcome to the big league.' Personally I didn't know whether to smile or wince."*

"When I saw Gary on Top Of The Pops I was very proud of him," revealed Lurkers drummer Peter Haynes, *"I knew he had something and we knew in The Lurkers that eventually Gary was going to do something with himself so to see him there was just great really. I remember looking at the audience on TOTP thinking that these kids had never seen him before and they didn't know that years earlier he'd been in a little punk band just chugging along in a burnt out van so yeah I was proud of him. Technology was entering everyday life and I think Gary and the music he was making just reflected the dehumanisation of our culture. I thought all that electronic stuff was very pioneering and it was quite amazing to me because I knew Gary and I knew him as a very ordinary and down to earth sort of bloke."*

Billie Currie also has vivid memories from this period: *"One minute the band are carting the gear up two flights of stairs in South East London, a place where Beggars Banquet had stuck us and nobody gives a* *f*** about you, the next minute you're Number One. Just seeing the effect that that has on a band, I mean I'd never seen that before and it was certainly interesting."*

What Numan managed to achieve was perfect synchronisation, the voice, the look, the sound, the subject matter, all of it fitting together like unplanned but perfect destiny. 'Are 'Friends' Electric?' revelled sonically with a far richer and fuller sound than could be found on many of the other synths available at the time and according to some synthesiser historians, this was possibly due to faulty ladder filters that modified the Minimoog and Polymoog synthesisers' outputs.

'Are 'Friends' Electric?' dominated the top spot during the summer making Thursday night's *Top Of The Pops* episode essential viewing for Gary's growing army of supporters. However, although the public were clearly enthralled with the whole Numan persona it wasn't without some noticeable dissent, as Gary later explained, *"The public got it before the media did, 'Are 'Friends' Electric?' was No.1 for two weeks before Radio 1 even decided to put it on the playlist."*

Unfortunately, Radio 1 and an increasingly hostile British pop press weren't the only stumbling blocks that Gary began to encounter, *"I remember turning up at TOTP once when 'Are 'Friends' Electric?' was at No. 1 and the band Squeeze were there. I went bowling in and said 'Hello everybody' and two of the band members, Glenn Tilbrook and Chris Difford basically made it clear that they were not all that keen on me. I think they'd been hovering at No. 2 or No. 3 at the time 'Are 'Friends' Electric?' had been No.1 and they just thought I was a bit of an upstart who'd nipped in and stolen their golden prize of a Number One. I was a bit surprised, especially with me being friendly, so that was my very first taste of professional rivalry."*

Andy McClusky of OMD also expressed his own simmering irritation when faced with the sudden appearance of Tubeway Army, *"Initially we were quite perturbed because people like ourselves, Cabaret Voltaire and The Human League had all just got used to the fact that we existed and then along comes this guy from London who's on the telly having a massive hit record!"*

In all, 'Are 'Friends' Electric?' spent four weeks at No.1, selling close to half a million copies with parent album *Replicas* joining it for one week on 21st July. The sheer scale and the speed of the band's success clearly came as quite a shock to Gary, as he later explained.

"One day you're sitting at home and nobody knows you. The next day you're in a toilet with Brian Ferry standing next to you waiting to do a TV show. 'Oh, hello!' you go. It's such a huge change, and people kind of expect you to take it in your stride, as though it's just another day. And it isn't. It's everything you ever dreamed of. More than you ever dreamed

of and only half as good. I became No.1 the second time I ever went on the telly, so I'd never learned about TV cameras, I'd never learned how to handle shows, interviews. In fact, I'd never even done an interview (except for a fanzine) when I got famous, then all of a sudden, I was talking to The Sun, The Melody Maker and all these people and I didn't have a clue how to do it. I thought Replicas would make me an interesting cult figure, I didn't dream that it would do what it did. I thought it might make it possible for me to become well thought of in musical circles. Boy was I wrong! My music literally went from being a hobby to becoming a multi-million pound business in a few months!"

CHAPTER 19
THE END IS ONLY THE BEGINNING...

"Isn't it strange how times change, I can't imagine living any other way"

(Lyric taken from 'Praying To The Aliens')

A minor spoiler to the celebratory atmosphere following the simultaneous No.1 successes of 'Are 'Friends' Electric?' and *Replicas,* was the sudden reappearance in June of the people behind the Lee Cooper jeans TV commercial, for which Gary had previously provided vocals. Following what seemed like a miraculous change of heart, the team now wanted Gary to sing the whole song that had featured in the television ad, with a view to releasing it as a single. However, having been treated so appallingly during the original recording session for 'Don't Be A Dummy' and also deliberately underpaid for it, Gary flatly refused to entertain the idea.

"When the advert was a success," recalled Numan, *"and I was a success, these people started to see that they could make some money out of it. I remembered the way it'd been, so I wouldn't do it. And I got a memo from WEA at that time saying that they would consider it a personal favour. Imagine a director saying he would consider it a personal favour if I did it. They were earning millions and millions out of me and I wouldn't do it. He (Ronnie Bond) wasn't very nice to me when I was a nothing and they'd obviously turned me over, so I said, 'No.' I certainly didn't need the money. It would have been putting a single out purely to make money out of people and take advantage of people who'd bought my own single and I didn't think that was very fair either. I hadn't written the song so at the time, I wasn't particularly keen on putting out something that I hadn't written anyway. I quite enjoyed being around to say 'sod off' when they came back to me."*

'Don't Be A Dummy' was eventually released as a single featuring ex-Atomic Rooster singer John Du Cann on vocals in place of Gary. The result was appalling, with Du Cann's vocal a laughable attempt at imitation. The single barely made a dent on the charts, despite a spirited, albeit embarrassing performance on *Top Of The Pops*.

With Gary Numan now a legitimate star, he at last found himself in a position to exert full control over his affairs. This began with settling a number of old scores, mainly with his former friends in and around the Mean Street crowd. He explained to journalist Paul Morley in the late spring of 1979, as 'Are 'Friends' Electric?' began its rapid ascent up the UK singles chart, *"There's a lot of people who I haven't forgotten, who were unkind to me. Now I'm in the charts and on the telly I sort of smile inside, knowing that they're watching. I'm waiting for them to ring up, 'oh do you remember me, I used to go around with you.'"*

In 1987, in conversation with Peter Gilbert, Gary went into greater detail about the motives behind his vengeful actions back in the spring of 1979, as his star began to rise. *"When I first got famous I went round to every old friend that had ever f***ed me over or every girlfriend that had ever dumped me, and sometimes the girlfriends of the blokes who had f**ked me over too, and just sorted everybody out in one way or another. I spent a week doing it. I got everyone. I left a trail of carnage and disillusionment behind me and I know it was pathetic, and I know it was extremely small-minded, but I didn't give a f**k. It was one of the best days of my life, best weeks of my life. You know they say that revenge is a very bad emotion. Bollocks, it's excellent."*

In the meantime Beggars Banquet found themselves once again in conflict with their newly born star when they reintroduced the idea of a club tour and began to set up dates around the country. *"I was really annoyed about it."* explained Gary, *"First of all because they hadn't asked me. Nick was keen on me to go out and do a club tour and I was violently opposed to doing any such thing until the money came in. He and I had a couple of stand-up rows about it. I don't remember Martin saying much about it one way or the other. It was obvious that we were becoming famous, and extremely quickly. I thought I'm not going to go out to do a club tour. I wanted do a proper concert tour with an enormous stage set and light show, the best show in the world."*

Though Gary faced strong opposition from Nick Austin, the club tour idea was eventually shelved. During the late summer, Gary finally laid the Tubeway Army name to rest for good, with the prolific singer delivering a third album that had been recorded back in the spring. This record completed his move away from guitars to an all encompassing electronic backdrop. Gary Numan's debut solo single, 'Cars', was released in September, hitting the top spot in the UK on the 22nd and joined by the album *The Pleasure Principle* that same week, giving him the rare accolade of scoring four consecutive No.1s and simultaneously topping both the singles and album charts, twice in succession.

A little earlier that week, on 20th September, the entire Gary Numan band along with the Beggars team had flown up to Glasgow to perform the first show of what became known as, *The Touring Principle*. What greeted Gary and the rest of the band at the Glasgow Apollo that evening as the curtains opened, was nothing short of complete teen hysteria. *"The show was great,"* enthused Mills, *"in fact it was almost unbelievable! It was then that we realised the scale of it at that Glasgow concert. We'd seen record sales on a computer printout but it was the* first time Gary or any of us had seen what fever there was out there. The kids were going wild and it was really exciting. Afterwards we were all backstage waiting to go back to the hotel when someone opened the stage door to where the bus was expected to be sitting. Instead there was literally a tidal wave of fans pushing up against the door. We were completely unprepared for this. We had to pull the door shut and re-group while we got some security to make way for us to get to the bus. I remember driving off down the road with all these fans running behind us banging on the windows."

There is little doubt that the synthesizer-heavy, post-punk songs on *Replicas* including 'Me! I Disconnect From You', 'Down In The Park' and of course the groundbreaking hit 'Are 'Friends' Electric?' were the catalyst for a synth-pop revolution that would echo throughout the 1980s and beyond. For Gary though, with four No.1 hits under his belt, his records selling in their millions, a sold-out world tour ahead of him and news that his music was climbing the charts in other countries around the globe, his rock 'n' roll odyssey was only just beginning…

GARY NUMAN
THE LAST WORD

"I think I became a success because at the time there was an overwhelming shortage of heroes. It was all bands. I honestly believed people wanted one person and that suited me. There was though, a tremendous kind of resistance to synthesizers, people thought it was quirky, here today, gone tomorrow. I've never claimed to be an original at the music, I was simply the first to make it famous and at the time I felt like I was waving my flag, fighting for a cause. But now I look back on it, and I think very differently.

I have very happy memories of all of that time. Pretty much everything that happened in 1979 was though, startling to me. It was just one massive thing after another. It felt exciting but dangerous, like a tornado, everything spinning by so fast you could barely register what it was, before it was gone and replaced by something else. The pressure was enormous and to be honest, I was out of my depth the entire time.

I was convinced that electronic music was my future and where music was going and I really, really wanted to be a part of it. Martin Mills at Beggars agreed and I have nothing but gratitude for Martin. When I started, there were only four of us on the label; it was like a little family. It was such a lovely way to start out, we were all learning, Martin hadn't had any success as a label so we were all kind of basking in that early success together and it was an amazing time. I wish I could have enjoyed it more when it was happening. The trouble was, I was already worrying about what I was going to do next. I was only half enjoying it.

As for the scene itself, I'm just glad that it's evolved the way it has. I'm glad that the stuff I did in those days gets some recognition. I'm glad that the whole electronic thing found its feet and became a totally established part of music in general, and that it has been now for a good couple of decades or so. I think there's better music around because of it. The technology itself has come on leaps and bounds. It's made a dramatic contribution to music in general, and I'm just proud that I played a small part in that."

EPILOGUE

The arrival of new band members Chris Payne, Cedric Sharpley and later RRussell Bell in the spring of 1979, marked the beginning of the end for Paul Gardiner. The break up of the Lidyard, Numan and Gardiner axis was something that the talented bassist seemingly never recovered from, as he explained to Ray Coleman in 1982, *"He (Gary) had to get those new players in, he had to do it, I know that, but something died for me, it seemed the end of the most important part of it all, making a success from the difficult beginning."*

Despite Paul's sadness at the loss of the original band nucleus he remained at Gary's side for a further two years before drifting away in 1981, following Numan's lavish farewell concerts at Wembley Arena in April of that year.

Tragically Paul was found dead on 18th February, 1984 on a bench in Limetrees Park near his home in Northolt, Middlesex. He was just 25 years old.

Paul was cremated nine days later on 27th February at Breakspear Crematorium in Ruislip, Middlesex. He is survived by his wife, Annette and his son, Chris.

Authors note:

Towards the conclusion of the writing process for this manuscript I was fortunate enough to strike up a friendship via social media with Annette Gardiner, the widow of Paul Gardiner, and it's during our exchanges that I mentioned this project. Annette was keen to set the record straight about Paul, noting that all the biographies on the internet are mostly incorrect, particularly the details surrounding his passing. Writing the following epitaph can't have been easy for Annette. I remain humbly honoured that Annette would grant permission for her memories of Paul and Gary to be published here for the very first time.

In Memory of Paul Gardiner
By Annette Gardiner - November 2014

"If you understand and research an addict's life, you begin to understand that they are not themselves when they're without the drugs on which they become so dependent. This is the sad paradox. Gary spoke to Paul during those times and clearly had a better insight to how Paul acted and reacted than most people. What he didn't realise though, was the day to day process in trying to get Paul clean. It was my Dad and I who bore the strain, getting him into rehab, taking him to see doctors. Every week, I went with him. I was ill myself, I had post-natal depression after my son was born in 1980 which didn't help the situation. Gary, Tony, Beryl and John all helped as much as they could. From memory, all of the members of the Webb family were so incredibly lovely.

When I first met Paul in 1977, he was at a friend's house listening to music, stoned on grass. He was the kind to dabble; he smoked weed but I didn't, although I did smoke cigarettes. I admit that I tried it once and remember Paul saying, 'It won't kill you.' From then on we both dabbled a little; we'd go to London, once a week, off and on. They were our young experimental times. Neither of us used anything but cannabis and I've not touched it or anything else for many years.

Paul moved in with me when I fell pregnant with our baby, in 1979. There was a lot going on at that time with, 'Are 'Friends' Electric?' getting to No.1. None of us realized it at the time because of everything going on around us, but Paul's addiction was spiralling. You see, Paul had a naturally addictive personality. I know all of this now, but I didn't then.

Paul kept a lot inside and I didn't know what he was doing while he was away on tour. I was fearful because I couldn't keep an eye on him, something I was able to do when we were together, much to Paul's displeasure because he knew I would try to keep him from getting drugs. He tried so hard to come off of it, only to be drawn back into it by the people who supplied it. Those dealers are the lowest of the low, they're rats.

Once, he called me, needing a shoulder to cry on and that's when it really first hit me that he had a problem. I wondered why his mood swings were becoming more frequent. He made a reverse charge call to my Mum's number and said he needed help. He was delusional, thinking he had the Mafia after him. He couldn't get drugs and told me he thought that because he'd found drugs to get him on stage that night, that they were after him. That bill was paid for by Tony, it was for well over a grand. Bless that man.

Paul and I decided to get a band together sometime around 1981/1982. Paul was into Lou Reed, Velvet Underground and other similar bands and we listened to music and started to write lyrics. Paul would write lyrics and ask me what I thought and I would sometimes give input. Another friend played guitar, Paul had a drum machine and Gary gave him a porta-studio to record on. Paul really wanted to rehearse so we found a drummer - he wanted the old school 'drums, bass, guitar' with keyboards as an atmospheric touch. We even did a gig under Paul's name at Uxbridge's Brunel University, which went down well. That is, apart from at the show's end when the drummer and side drummer, another long time friend of Paul's, ended up fighting! Paul had said the side drummer could join us to improvise alongside the main drummer. This was a mistake in my mind but luckily the fight broke out after the last song!

I tried my best to help Paul, and there were many arguments. I was also being prescribed medication for anxiety and my doctor put me on Valium, an awful drug which I eventually weaned myself off. I took Paul to a doctor every Friday and I saved him on at least two occasions from an overdose. Sadly when we lost our flat in 1983, and following advice from the social workers, we had to go and live in separate locations. The idea was that if we lived separately, there would be more chance of getting a new place from the council. I also had our son, Chris, so there was a better chance that I would get the first option. But we always kept in touch and Paul agreed to go along with this and then decide on which flat we would live in. Paul was staying in Ealing and I was in Harrow. Paul died on his way round to see Chris and I in February, 1984. Paul didn't die from any street drugs. What actually killed him, was an overdose of prescribed medication and alcohol. There was simply too much of both in his system and this, coupled with the heavy snow that year, plunged the temperature down to below zero that night. He couldn't survive it.

Paul just found himself in a terrible place in his life but throughout all of those difficulties, I've never stopped loving him. There were times I felt like running away myself. I could have left, I could have walked away but it didn't ever enter my head because Paul was the kindest, sweetest person you could ever hope to meet, and our lives were soured by drugs. I loved Paul to the end and if I could have done so, I would have willingly taken the pain for him."

LIVE HISTORY:

Early 1977

Performance as Riot at Crackers night club
Performance as Heroin at Stanwell Hall
Performance as Stiletto at Ashfield College

AS THE LASERS:

26th June   The Roxy
                Unknown date in June at Bones in Reading

AS TUBEWAY ARMY:

1977

22nd Jul	The Roxy
10th Sep	The Roxy
15th Sep	The Roxy
1st Oct	The Roxy
6th Dec	The Vortex (band signed to Beggars Banquet Records following this showcase)
12th Dec	Oriel Youth Centre, Northolt

(Unknown date and performance with Adam And The Antz, speculated to be one of the following four dates: 16th Dec, 1977 (The Roxy) / 7th Jan, 1978 (The Roxy) / 21st Jan, 1978 (The Roxy) or 22nd April, 1978 (Rochester Castle, Stoke Newington)

1978

28th Jan	Rochester Castle
4th Feb	Dingwalls
5th Feb	The Marquee
9th Feb	Ashford Grammar School in Middlesex
19th Feb	The Marquee
21st Feb	The Rock Garden
24th Feb	The Corn Exchange
7th Mar	The Vortex
10th Mar	Dingwalls
18th Mar	Uxbridge
3rd April	The Vortex

17th Apr	Upstairs At Ronnie Scott's
20th Apr	The Marquee
1st May	Bones Reading
	The Royal Holloway College Egham
	Wraysbury (unknown venue)
2nd Jun	Hayes
17th Jun	The Windsor Castle
	The Hope and Anchor
28th Jun	The White Hart

Cancelled show:
5th July at a local pub called The Brooke House in Hayes, Middlesex with label-mates The Doll.

Six further venues and support slots where Tubeway Army are rumoured to have performed. No information available at present:

The Pegasus Stoke Newington
The YMCA Galaxy Club Harlow now the Square
The Royal Hotel Luton
Greenford Hall Ealing
Local scout club Wraysbury
Support slot for Sham 69 sometime in 1978

Before Gary Numan there was Tubeway Army, and before Tubeway Army there was Gary Webb, a determined and ambitious 16 year old singer/songwriter from West London, who in the punk-assaulted summer of 1976, dispensed with full time education to pursue his long held dream of fame and stardom.

To assist him in this quest came talented bassist, Paul Gardiner with whom Gary first founded Tubeway Army. Together with Gary's uncle, drummer Gerald Lidyard, they gigged sporadically around central London as the band eventually drew the attention of a small independent record label, Beggars Banquet.

Gary Numan   Paul Gardiner

No-one could have predicted back then that in just a few short months, music history was about to be made as Gary Numan and Tubeway Army burst onto the music scene in the early summer of 1979 with the futuristic anthem "Are 'Friends' Electric?', a song that ushered in a fresh and exciting new era in popular music.

Printed in Poland
by Amazon Fulfillment
Poland Sp. z o.o., Wrocław